EXIT RICH BEYOND MONEY

Cashing Out on Your Life's Work and Living Your Ideal Life

Noah Rosenfarb, CPA & Peter Culver, JD
Founders of Freedom Family Office

EXIT RICH BEYOND MONEY: Cashing Out on Your Life's Work and Living Your Ideal Life

Copyright © 2024 by Noah Rosenfarb, CPA and Peter Culver, JD.
Published by Better Life Books, Inc.

All rights are reserved. No part of this publication may be reproduced, stored in a retrieval system, or transmitted in any form or by any means, electronic, mechanical, photocopying, recording, or otherwise, without prior permission of the publisher. The only exception is brief quotations in printed reviews.

Special discounts are available on quantity purchases by organizations. Requests for more information can be emailed to Hello@freedomfamilyoffice.com.

To the entrepreneurs who dared to dream,

Who took risks in the face of uncertainty,

Who invested not only in ideas but in people,

And who created something of value that enriched the lives of others.

You are the true heroes of our time.

This book is for you.

CONTENTS

Introduction: Why You Must Read This Book vii
Chapter 1: The Five Core Tenets of Exit Planning............................1
Chapter 2: What's My Business Worth? 9
Chapter 3: What's Your Number?..15
Chapter 4: What Am I Going to Do With Myself?............................23
Chapter 5: How Will a Transfer or Sale Affect My Family? 27
Chapter 6: Building the Transition Team 33
Chapter 7: Choosing an Exit Strategy..41
Chapter 8: Five Essential Areas to Prepare for Transition 53
Chapter 9: Company Management Through Transition 65
Chapter 10: Developing Clear Money Intentions 73
Chapter 11: Building Your Legacy..81
Chapter 12: Navigating the World of Financial Advice 89
Chapter 13: Where Do I Go From Here?...99
About the Authors...101

BONUS CHAPTERS 105
Chapter 14: Changing the Odds of Family Wealth Transfers..........107
Chapter 15: Lessons Learned From Buying and
Selling Companies..113
Chapter 16: 53 Ways to Make Your Business More Valuable 125
10 Key Steps for Your Perfect Exit..235
Top 10 Mistakes After Your 8-Figure Exits....................................236
10 Critical Before You Exit Questions to Answer 237
Future Considerations 239
Resources for Readers 243

Introduction

WHY YOU MUST READ THIS BOOK

"A Journey of a thousand miles begins with a single step."

— CHINESE PROVERB

Every business owner needs to have an answer to this question:

How do you want to leave your business?

It's a great question. Unfortunately, many owners don't have an answer at all, let alone a great answer. For over 40 years, we have served as trusted advisors to business owners preparing for a sale or transfer. Based on our experience, expertise, and research, we created this book to:

1. Build awareness of the value that can be produced by proactively creating a thoughtful, strategic, and realistic exit plan.

2. Provide the framework to create your exit plan and evaluate your preparedness.

3. Encourage you to collaborate with a multi-disciplined team

with the knowledge and resources to identify and transform your goals into an effective and actionable exit plan.

You Are Not Alone

Baby boomers today are still one of the largest and most entrepreneurial generations in United States history. As of 2023, they own approximately 40% of privately held small businesses in the United States, or 2.34 million businesses with employees. These businesses employ nearly 25 million people, highlighting the substantial impact of boomer-owned businesses on the job market and economy. Over the next 20 years, a large wave of business owners will be reaching retirement age and will ultimately need an exit from the management and/or ownership of their companies. This will be the largest ownership transfer in U.S. history, and, as such, begs the questions: will this create a heavily skewed buyer's market, and what can I do to accomplish my business, personal, family, and financial goals?

The answer is that you need to start strategically thinking about your goals so you can understand how to best plan your exit to achieve them. When do you want to exit? Who will take over your responsibilities? How do you want to exit—in one event or over time? Who will be there to buy your interest? How are they going to pay you? Will your business provide enough income to fulfill your long-term personal financial needs? What will you do with your time post-exit?

If you cannot answer these questions, you are not alone. You are part of the 87% of owners who do not have an exit plan or the 80% of owners who have given this matter little to no attention.

As an exit-planning advisor, it is shocking that when those same private business owners are asked if they think it is important to have an exit plan, 90% say yes. Worse, for those owners that do exit, 75% express regret, stating that their exit did not accomplish their goals. All told, these are really terrible statistics—everybody will ultimately need to exit, nobody's planning for it, and once they get out, they regret not planning for it.

Planning Roadblocks

Most owners avoid exit planning for one or more of the following reasons:

- You don't want to think about leaving.

- You think it's too early to start planning.

- You're too busy putting out fires.

- You don't know where to begin.

- You don't have an advisor that is knowledgeable in this specialized field.

- You have difficulty discussing financial, family, and/or personal matters with anyone.

- The process just seems too daunting.

The field of exit planning has evolved to address these roadblocks. Exit planning has now become a recognized area of expertise, and many advisors have now focused on helping owners overcome these challenges and avoid seller's remorse.

What is Exit Planning?

There are four critical areas one needs to ask and answer questions in to have a complete exit plan. Here are just a few questions to help you get in the right frame of mind:

- **Business**—What should I do today to maximize the value of my business? Can my business be sold for a price I would accept?

- **Personal**—When do I want to exit? Following my exit, how will I spend my days? How will my sense of self and identity be affected?

- **Family**—Which family members should be included in the sale decisions? How can my exit positively impact each family member?

- **Financial**—How much money do I need to live the life I envision? What might I do to minimize future taxes?

Failing to Plan

A majority of owners who sold their company say, "I made a mistake." Do you know their biggest regret? Selling their company did not accomplish their personal or financial goals. When asked why, most business owners said they did not fully understand all their options or the process. When asked what they would do differently if they could do it all over again, they said they would have been better prepared. Only after a transaction do most owners realize that they should have made planning a priority. We hope that this book will prompt you to take action and avoid the same fate.

There are numerous reasons to have an exit plan, not the least of which are the five big Ds:

- Death
- Divorce
- Disability
- Disputes
- Distress

If you were "hit by a bus" yesterday, your death would change the world for your family, your employees, and your customers. One of the ideas behind having an answer to this question of how you will leave your business is to put a plan in place for the people who are left behind. It is too common that tragedy strikes a business owner and, without a moment's notice, employees and customers start leaving. Spouses and children who are left with a business that their loved ones invested a lot of time, energy, effort, and money in are left with nothing. That is an unfortunate consequence of the failure to plan.

Divorce is an incredibly common occurrence in modern society. 50% of families that start in marriage end in divorce, and divorce rates increase with subsequent marriages. A lot of baby boomer business owners are on their second or third marriages, making it even more important to take a look at what would happen in the event of a divorce.

How would your company pay your spouse their entitlement for their share of your company's value? What about paying alimony out of the cash flow from your company?

Maybe you are secure in your own marriage, but what about your partners or your children who may share ownership now or will share ownership in the future?

Divorce can be devastating to a business and cripple it for years, so it's important to understand the impact. Educating yourself about the consequences of divorce helps address all the types of planning that you might implement around these five big Ds. It will help put you in a better position to have a company that will create lasting value that will live beyond your own work efforts.

When an owner can't show up for work for months at a time due to a disability, businesses often fall apart. Having a plan in place not only helps keep the business running and healthy but also ensures that the family bills are getting paid.

Without a doubt, disputes happen in companies all the time. But when a dispute occurs among owners, it can be most problematic. It is important to understand what you would do in the event of a partnership dispute. There are agreements you can enter into now, processes that can be established, and other issues that must be explored.

The last big D, distress, is an overall catchphrase to describe what happens in any of these or other scenarios when you have significant pressure placed on the business, the owner, or the management team, making it difficult to keep up.

Let's take a look at the consequences of this failure to plan. It's important to look at the consequences to motivate you to take action.

Certainly, a significant consequence is that you will receive less value for the business that you have worked so hard to build. That's not the idea of business. One reason for going into business is to create cash flow to provide for yourself and your family. Beyond the cash flow and the benefits to your community and your employees, there is typically a goal of creating an exit in which you will get value for the business that you've created.

> Look at exit planning as a way of maximizing the return on your biggest investment; a way of creating peace of mind for your family, your employees and yourself; all by simply having a data-driving well-thought-out plan.

Benefits of Exit Planning

Let's change direction and talk about the benefits of planning.

Options: A key element of exit planning is it provides you with options. This means making sure that you can transfer the company on your terms and in the manner you want, whether to family members, your management team, or an outside buyer at the highest price. When you plan, you are gaining the flexibility and the freedom to choose the path you want. Without planning, it's hard to know if you're really going to get where you want to be or if you will maintain control.

Maximizing Value: An exit plan will help you maximize the value of your company by reducing business risks and increasing future profits. That not only enhances your business value but also typically increases what you earn while you remain the owner.

Family Harmony and Wealth: Similarly, if you're looking at one of the ways to preserve your family wealth for later generations, exit planning can have one of the best returns on investment. We're not just suggesting estate planning strategies, which are important; we're talking about looking at the interplay between company ownership among family members and management and between family owners who work in the business and those who do not. Relationship issues tend to be complex and become a source of disputes. By opening the lines of communication and proactively putting a plan in place, you can avoid some of the common problems that occur when family-owned businesses are transferred between generations.

Contingency Plan: Perhaps one of the best benefits of planning is giving your employees and your family confidence that no matter what happens to you, they are going to be okay.

Tax: Another significant element of planning is to eliminate, minimize, or defer company, personal, and estate taxes. One of the clear benefits of planning is looking at some tax reduction strategies so that you can keep more of what's yours.

Time and Timing

Great exit planning takes up to 2 years, as business value enhancements, tax planning, market timing, and the sale or transition process all need to be strategically mapped out, implemented, and aligned. It does require a commitment. Every hour of planning can create value beyond that of what you can get just working in your business and putting out fires. It is, without a doubt, one of the greatest ways to invest your time.

When business owners were asked how much time they spent working on a deal before they actually sold their company, the average was an astounding 1,500 hours. The reality is that you are going to spend the time transferring ownership of your company whether it is to your family, to your management team, or a third party.

It becomes a question of when you want to spend the time. Do you want to spend it a little bit at a time over the next 2 to 5 years, 5 to 10 years, or even 6 months? Or are you ready to wait until the pressure builds and the unforeseen happens in your life? One day, you may decide, "Today's the day I have to get out," and all of a sudden, you have to face all of the issues that must be addressed in order to transfer your company.

Just Do It

The answer is clear. Look at exit planning as a way of maximizing the return on your biggest investment; a way of creating peace of mind for your family, your employees, and yourself; all by simply having a data-driven, well-thought-out, and strategic answer to the question:

How do you want to leave your business?

CHAPTER 1

THE FIVE CORE TENETS OF EXIT PLANNING

"Big changes usually happen through a series of smaller steps, and big decisions are taken only after intermediate steps are tried and found wanting."

— BRAD SESTER

The succession or exit of a business owner is usually the single largest financial transaction in their lifetime. Often, there is only one chance to get it done properly. Accordingly, an owner needs to be well-prepared to begin the exit planning process about 2 years before a desired exit. Business value enhancements, tax planning, market timing, and the sale or transition process itself all need time to be strategically mapped out, implemented, and aligned.

A true and properly prepared exit plan offers the following five core tenets for an owner.

1. **Aligning an Owner's Business, Personal, Family, and Financial Goals**

Determining the success or failure of an owner's exit is defined and measured differently by every business owner. Accordingly, the first step of any exit or succession plan should always be the articulation and alignment of the owner's goals. This exercise creates the necessary underpinning foundation of the plan and equips the owner and their advisors with a compass to proficiently navigate a successful exit.

To begin, an owner needs to answer the following goal questions:

- **Business**—What should I do today to maximize the value of my business? Can my business be sold for a price I would accept?

- **Personal**—When do I want to exit? Following my exit, how will I spend my days? How will my sense of self and identity be affected?

- **Family**—Which family members should be included in the sale decisions? How can my exit positively impact each family member?

- **Financial**—How much money do I need to live the life I envision? What might I do to minimize the taxes I may pay in the future?

Really Ask Yourself...

How many hours do you want to spend working? Where would you like to live, and in what kind of housing? How often are you traveling, and how do you get there? We work with families who envision spending as little as $25,000 a month, and others who want to own multiple homes, fly private, stay at high-end resorts, and enjoy "the finer things" while spending $250,000 a month. It's all about you and your goals.

Once you have identified your goals, the next step is to reconcile all goals into alignment. This is necessary because certain aspects of each of the individual goals may not match with one another. For example, many owners have a financial goal (e.g., sell for $50M) and a timeframe goal (e.g., be out by my 66th birthday). If these two are incapable of being achieved together, you have to prioritize which is more important.

The key to prioritizing is recognizing which goals are flexible and which must be achieved. Long-term, personal, and financial needs generally have limited flexibility, and this usually drives prioritization. Sound financial data, including the amount required to meet your personal long-term financial needs, needs to be benchmarked to the amount your ownership is worth under various goal scenarios and other what-if scenarios. When completing this process, owners need to be aware that there are outside market influences they have no control over, so all goals should be set with some flexibility.

2. **Empowering an Owner With an In-Depth Knowledge of All Their Succession or Exit Options**

To satisfy an owner's business, personal, family, and financial goals, a sound exit plan evaluates all the options and alternatives and vets each to determine the optimal solution for the owner. This process is normally completed in conjunction with the reconciliation of an owner's goals process, as just explained above. As presented below, there are typically eight major exit channels.

> If you take a dollar and double it five times tax-free, you'd have $32. With just a 25% tax levied every time you double your money, you'd end up with just $16. A 25% tax can make a huge difference in your overall exit outcome.
>
> When you have a seven-figure income, or an eight-figure exit, those differences add up!

Determining the availability of the different exit channels is dependent upon the underlying company's profile (ownership structure, entity type, size, profitability, maturity, outlook, etc.). The desirability of each exit channel is based on the motivations and goals of the owner. After narrowing the list for both factors (availability and desirability), the range of options becomes clear.

Here is a summary of exit channels, along with a brief description of the pros and cons. We dive deeper into each exit option in Chapter 7.

External Exit Channels	Internal Exit Channels
- Financial Buyer - Strategic Buyer (Vertical/Horizontal) - Initial Public Offering (IPO)	- Recapitalization Family - Co-owner(s) Management Employees (ESOP)
Pros - Generally highest available value diversification of a family's wealth - Post-sale financial and leadership resources	**Pros** - Greater control over legacy, timing, and terms - Income and estate tax saving opportunities - Limited due diligence and time required to close
Cons - Time and cost of marketing, due diligence, and closing transaction - Limited control over post-legacy value	**Cons** - IRS and tax courts are value authorities for family and ESOP transfers - The value received is often less than the actual market value - Buyer's financial resources are usually limited

3. Maximizing the Fundamental Value of the Business

Buyers look at numerous aspects of a company to determine value—not just how much a company earns. To maximize value, owners must be able to view their company from a buyer's perspective. What would you expect or look for if you were making an acquisition?

Thus, a sound exit plan should evaluate the company from a buyer's perspective. In this process, you identify opportunities to increase the underlying company's value, and then develop and implement action plans to achieve these goals before exiting. Assessing the opportunities is often hard to do from an insider's perspective, especially if an owner does not have experience with buying or selling companies. Wise owners seek outside perspectives that have merger and acquisition experience.

Chapter 16, "53 Ways to Make Your Business More Valuable," is an excellent tool to use as you begin your journey. We provide a scoring framework that helps owners efficiently assess, prioritize, and implement value enhancements at their company. Owners should start working on the value-building processes 2 to 5 years before a transfer, as implementation of enhancements takes time. Should you choose to stay engaged with the business longer than initially planned, the value enhancements will have created a stronger and smoother running company for you to enjoy.

4. Eliminating, Minimizing, or Deferring Income and Estate Taxes

The actual value realized by an owner is always less than the company's selling price; it is the culmination of the price, structure, terms, and the corresponding tax consequences of the sale. The amount of the tax component continues to shock owners. There are multiple tax-saving opportunities that a good exit plan addresses, but they all require advanced planning.

There are four tiers of tax planning, which we highlight throughout the book:

1. Company entity level
2. Personal level
3. Estate level
4. Transaction level

At the transaction level, the structure of the deal can result in a difference of up to 40% in net proceeds for an owner. Expertise, creativity, and analysis need to be completed before going to market in order to determine the best structure and deal strategy available for the owner.

5. **Maximizing What the Market Is Willing to Pay for the Business**

The last core tenet of a good exit plan is for the 80% of owners that elect an external transfer channel. Maximizing what the market is willing to pay is different from maximizing the fundamental value, as we are specifically focusing on how the sale process can work in favor of an owner. There are four main ways to do this.

1. **Sell-side due diligence ("mock due diligence")**—This is a process of conducting the same intensive review as a buyer would conduct. It requires compiling and/or organizing the documentation a buyer would request in advance (typically in an online data room) and requires that qualified professionals review the documents/data to uncover any issues or opportunities. One benefit of the process is that it expedites the actual due diligence a buyer will conduct. This helps prevent confidentiality issues, minimizes operating distractions, helps assure the deal will close, and gets the deal closed sooner. Another benefit is that it prevents the deal from going sideways or getting canceled altogether. Too often, the skeletons come out of the closet during due diligence. If the seller is aware of potential problems, then the seller can address the issues or make the buyer aware of them in advance.

The Five Core Tenets of Exit Planning

2. **Market timing**—As all business owners know, timing is everything. To realize and maximize ownership value, all of the critical market, company, personal, and tax elements must be aligned. This is a dynamic process with the critical market elements being outside an owner's control. The windows of sale opportunities open and close based on economic conditions and the cycles of industries and market segments. For that reason, the goal of a good exit plan is to complete all the value enhancements, tax planning, individual wealth planning, preparedness, etc. so the owner is in a state of readiness and agility, equipped to capitalize on the market windows of opportunities as they present themselves.

3. **Competing buyers**—Experienced merger and acquisition professionals always say, 'One buyer is no buyer.' Accordingly, as part of an exit plan, an ideal buyer profile should be created, and a list of potential buyers that match the profile should be developed. The list should contain both financial and strategic buyers.

4. **The sale/marketing approach**—There are two basic approaches available: a negotiated sale and a controlled auction. In simplified terms, the negotiated sale is where the seller performs limited marketing of the company and directly solicits interest from a few known potential buyers. The seller talks with each interested buyer on a first-come, first-served basis and attempts to negotiate the best deal. The controlled auction process casts a much wider net in its marketing process and follows a much more formal and structured process. The process begins with sending a "teaser" to a large list of potential interested buyers, followed by a detailed "offering memorandum" for those interested. A deadline to submit bids is then circulated. Based on the qualifying bids, the seller invites a handful of buyers for face-to-face meetings, touring the company and providing an opportunity to vet each other. After the visits, buyers have a deadline to submit final offers to purchase, and the best purchase offer is chosen by the seller. The controlled auction is the preferred method to create a competing buyers' environment, but it is an intensive and costly

process and is not appropriate for all companies.

These five core tenets of exit planning are the basis for tremendous value creation for owners.

They help align the financial side of a transfer not only on a quantitative basis but also reflect a series of qualitative issues that, when solved in advance, can be worth more than money.

Questions to Consider

- What do you want your business to accomplish before your exit?

  _____
  _____

- When do you want to exit?

  _____
  _____

- How do you want to exit—over time or in one event?

  _____
  _____

- Who do you want to exit to?

  _____
  _____

- What do you want to accomplish as part of your eventual exit?

  _____
  _____

- What are your long-term personal financial needs, and what is the amount you need from your business to accomplish them?

  _____
  _____

Chapter 2

WHAT'S MY BUSINESS WORTH?

> *"Every wealthy investor I know and every wealthy investor you know has either built their wealth through ownership or inherited it from an owner."*
>
> — ROLAND MANARIN

It's a question that might not have a correct answer until you actually receive money from someone else. There is one certainty: whatever you think your business is worth, a buyer will want to pay less. A buyer is always going to pressure the price down, and your job as a seller is always to establish reasons to keep the price up.

The science behind business valuation is incredibly complex but can be expressed in a rather basic way:

$$\frac{\text{Buyer's Future Benefit Stream (Cash Flow)}}{\text{Expected Rate of Return}}$$

There are clearly challenges in determining a "buyer's future benefit stream," not the least of which are predicting the future revenue and expenses for the company in the hands of the buyer. An evaluation of reasonable owner compensation, for which expenses paid by the company are not for business purposes (cars, trips, etc.), and many other factors come into play. For the "expected rate of return," the range varies widely based on size, buyer, company stage, interest rates, and more. A benchmark of expected rates of return can be found by viewing the Pepperdine Private Capital Markets Project's private cost of capital (PCOC) rates. Proxies for established private companies are private equity groups (PEG) as shown below.

Source Quartile	1st Quartile	Median	3rd Quartile
PEG ($1M EBITDA)	27.5%	30.0%	34.0%
PEG ($5M EBITDA)	25.0%	26.0%	30.0%
PEG ($10M EBITDA)	23.0%	25.0%	28.5%
PEG ($25M EBITDA)	22.5%	25.0%	28.0%
PEG ($50M EBITDA)	22.0%	24.0%	27.0%
PEG ($100M EBITDA)	22.0%	24.0%	25.0%

As an example, if your business produces $2M of cash flow (before personal income tax) and the desired rate of return is 25% (also referred to as a multiple of 4x), your business is worth $8M.

Another critical point in transition planning is taking a look at how much of your net worth is tied up in your business. In most cases, it is at least 70%. From our experience and viewing the above chart, we know the expected returns in the private equity marketplace (where people are acquiring businesses for profit and return on their investment) are generally 20% to 35% (3x to 5x multiples of cash flow). You as an owner should have the same expectations as the market regarding your current investment in your company. If your private business does not provide you with that type of return, it is a sign that your private company investment is not sufficient for the inherent risk you are taking.

In calculating your return on your private company investment, avoid using the cost of your investment, and instead use the prior period value of your investment. Using your actual investment cost is irrelevant because your initial investment is a sunk cost. Investment cost and value are two different measurements. Here, we are measuring the production of the investment, which is measured by the change in value.

Profit Increases = Value Enhancement

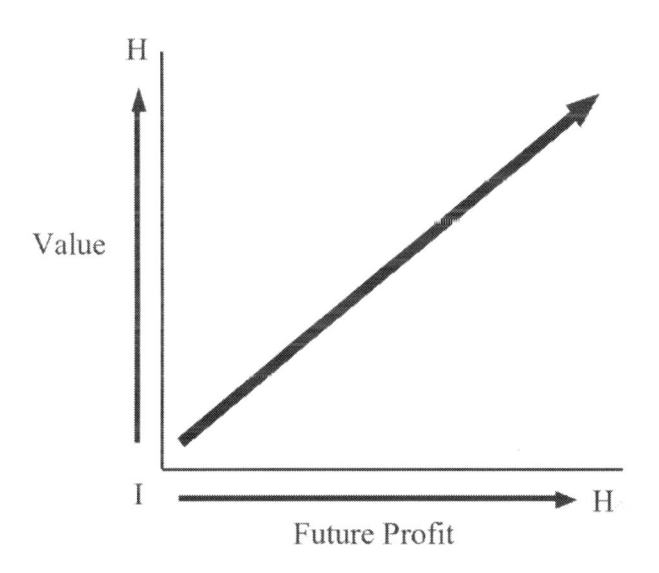

To make your business worth more, you have to create more value. There are only a few ways to create value in businesses. We can boil it down to two simple mathematical equations.

1. Increase future profits.
2. Decrease future risks.

Either of these will make your company more valuable. The key is deriving a plan to do one or both, and that's where business valuation enhancement activities make a lot of sense.

Risk Reduction = Value Enhancement

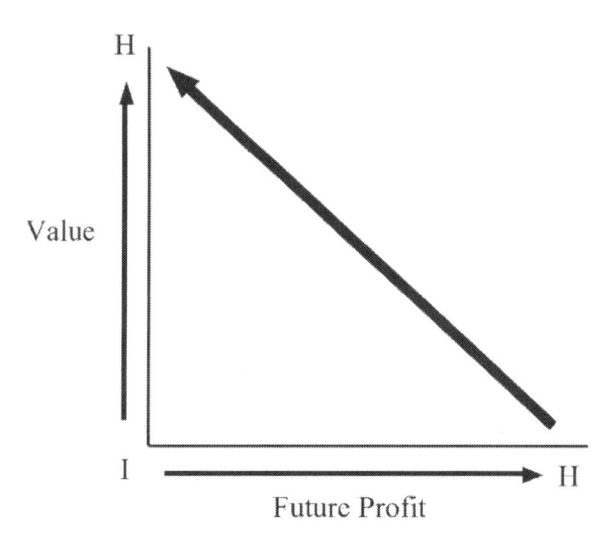

[Graph with Y-axis labeled "Value" ranging from L to H, and X-axis labeled "Future Profit" ranging from L to H, with a downward-sloping arrow from lower right to upper left]

Increasing the value of your business requires preparation, it requires action, and it clearly requires people. You need to have talented leadership, and you need to motivate them through incentives. They may not get the lion's share of the rewards for the profits they generate, but they need something. Most exit planning involves some type of performance-based compensation system that may include "golden handcuffs" so that buyers have confidence that the management team will stay in place after a transaction.

Of course, you need to examine your customers. Is it a growing customer base? Do your customers stay with you for a long time? What about customer concentration? If you have too much revenue derived from too few customers, that's a risk that you want to evaluate closely and see how you can minimize it. An exit plan evaluates this metric and can establish corrective actions if needed.

There may also be market opportunities that you want to pursue. You have to take a look at sales, margins, and growth opportunities. Then you need to start prioritizing them. Showing evidence that your team can plan, execute, and profit will both increase profits and decrease risks.

Financial reporting is another way to reduce risks for a buyer. If they have a good sense of comfort with the numbers that you create, the information that you provide, and the projections that you present, the buyer will perceive a reduced risk in acquiring your company. Things like timely key performance indicators that show the health of a company on the back of a napkin create tremendous value. Making sure that you have budgeted and actual results and monitoring the variance is also critical. If you have a statistical presentation for how well you do at your budget-to-actual ratio that covers a few years, you will build confidence in the buyer regarding the nature of your future projections.

Do you have audited financial statements? If not, buyers are going to want an audit to take place if the transaction is of significant value. As you can imagine, getting that audit done at the last minute for years that may have passed might be expensive, cumbersome, and time-consuming. Part of exit planning is taking a look at what you're going to need to reduce the risk to a buyer, and in financial reporting, there are many ways to reduce risk.

In the end, if you implement some of these business value enhancements and you prepare and execute, you're going to maximize your options. You're going to increase the future value of your company, and for the most part, it's going to increase your current income as well.

Planning will also minimize variations in the earning streams that you have. You'll decrease the risk even while you own the company, and you'll prevent yourself from having to deal with discounts that buyers want to take when making you offers.

So the fact is, it's not a question of whether you are going to exit your business; it's just a question of whether you're going to exit on your terms. The failure to do presale preparation is the number one reason deals fail.

In our practice, we encourage clients to take ample time to prepare. From our experience of helping clients through an exit, collaborating with an advisor can make the process go more smoothly and as stress-free as possible. An experienced exit planner will know how to lead you through each stage, hold the meetings that need to be held, gather your exit team, and create accountability metrics so that all the preparation is done successfully. Some work has to be done by outside advisors, some by the internal management team, and some by you and other owners.

By spreading the allocation of effort around a large network of committed people, what we find is that not only do we create great value in the company, but we also create an atmosphere of trust and camaraderie that leads to a better result for you while you remain the business owner.

Questions to Consider

- What are three ways you can increase profits before your exit?

  _____

  _____

- What are three risks a buyer might perceive that you can decrease or eliminate in the next year?

  _____

  _____

- If you plan to offer incentives to key employees, who will help you design and implement the plan?

  _____

  _____

- If you need to change your financial reporting, who will determine what needs to change and the cost to make those changes?

  _____

  _____

Chapter 3

WHAT'S YOUR NUMBER?

"Not everything that can be counted counts, and not everything that counts can be counted."

— Albert Einstein

How much money do you need to live a comfortable and secure retirement? The number varies for every family and every person. The reason it varies so widely is that we all have different expectations of what we want to spend, what we might need to spend, and how much extra money we need "just in case" to feel comfortable.

Let us describe that in more detail. A common way that people look at "the number" is to take 25 years' worth of annual spending. If you spend $250,000 per year, multiply that by 25. That gives you $6.25M. If you were to withdraw 4% every year for the rest of your life, you'd receive $250,000 annually. This is a very simple way to begin your calculation, but it puts you in the ballpark.

One problem is that you might think you need $250,000 now, but if you or your spouse were to become ill, you may need a lot more. So beyond the $6.25M needed to cover your current lifestyle, you might need another million dollars just to protect yourself from healthcare issues. A second family might say they don't need that million dollars for healthcare because they have a long-term care insurance policy. And yet another family might say they have three daughters who will certainly take care of them if needed. Each family's circumstances are different.

In reality, calculating a number is more cumbersome. You have to evaluate not just the expense side risks, but also your risk management program and your portfolio management. You have to take a look at the income needs of your family alongside your tax strategy and put them all together into a very different strategy than wealth accumulation planning. This is referred to as wealth utilization planning. Let us describe the difference.

There are four phases of wealth. The first phase is when you're a child and are dependent on others. There is no real wealth strategy other than dependency. There are no savings. There is really no income or expense other than maybe summer jobs or college earnings.

Once you become independent, and maybe after a few years of living paycheck to paycheck, you finally start a family, buy a house, and start saving for the future. This could include a college education, a summer home, or retirement. That's the wealth accumulation stage, which is the second phase of wealth. Most people are focused on this stage of planning in the financial services field. For wealth accumulation, people evaluate portfolios in a particular way.

Advisors make investment recommendations based on your continued ability to earn and save income, to withstand periods of market losses, and to accept certain risks because of these facts.

When it is time to utilize wealth, which is the third stage, planning has to change dramatically. In wealth utilization planning, there is a significant emotional aspect that has to be addressed between you and your advisor. It is important to gain an understanding of how you feel about money and what your relationship with the money that you've accumulated is going to look like. For many people who have been experts at wealth accumulation, wealth utilization is incredibly difficult.

What's Your Number?

Many challenges go along with seeing your account get depleted or stagnate as you utilize your wealth. You might be used to seeing your accounts grow. You may have measured regularly how much you contributed and how much the accounts grew from investment performance. Now here you are in the wealth utilization stage, with significant assets that you have created through your efforts, and it becomes gut-wrenching to see the withdrawals that have to come out.

That's one of the things that we focus on with our clients: helping them understand the change from wealth accumulation to wealth utilization.

Let us turn to talk a little bit about risk management and what that means. There are all sorts of risks when taking a look at your investments, but there are also risks in other areas as well. We'll list 15 risks to give you some examples.

1. The risk of inflation—prices will rise

2. Market volatility—the markets are going to go up and down and may be down when you need to use your money

3. Taxes, income, or estate taxes, and how that will impact the wealth you've accumulated

4. Premature death

5. Disability

6. Lawsuits

7. Longevity—what if you live until you're 110?

8. Loss of income

9. Property losses

10. Divorce

11. Overspending

12. Under saving

13. Misinformation—listening to people, news programs, or talking heads giving you incorrect information

14. Arrogance or pride—thinking that you know better

15. Procrastination

The reason we collaborate with clients is to avoid the significant risks that go along with procrastinating. We help clients get out of their own way and start a process to deal with each of these risks. If you have a plan, the risks are not that challenging. Neglecting to do anything will produce the worst outcome for you.

Portfolio management is another aspect of wealth utilization planning that is equally important to the risk management component. One of the ways that people look at portfolio management is to ask, "How can I get the smoothest sailing sea? What's the way to avoid volatility in my portfolio?" Unfortunately, that's not always the best strategy.

Volatility is critically important to equity markets and to owning companies. The ups and the downs—most people hate that feeling; it's like getting jerked around. What we suggest is to evaluate volatility in a different framework.

Most people define volatility as the risks of investments moving up or down on any particular day, week, or month and how big that movement might be in comparison to other potential investments. Measuring things by the day, week, or month is not a great strategy if you plan to utilize your assets over 10, 20, 30, or 40 years or more.

> One piece of advice I give is for clients to NOT sell their business unless they're making at least 20% of their desired lifestyle expenses from passive income.

What we recommend is to take an approach called bucketing. Instead of looking at the pool of assets you've accumulated as one pool of money to start drawing an income from, we break that money up into different buckets. Let's go back to the example of someone who needs $250,000 a year from a $6.25 million portfolio.

We might take $750,000 and put it in accounts that do not have volatility, whether they're certificates of deposit, cash accounts, savings bonds, or things that have nowhere to go but up, so to speak. The tradeoff is that your returns may be next to nothing. The benefit is that your next 3 years of expenses are covered.

Then we're looking at years 4 to 8, maybe even years 9 and 10. Let's say we can put away 7 years' worth of $250,000 amounts, another $1.75 million. While we know we don't need the money in the next 3 years, we do need it within the next 10. We might not want to expose that money to significant market volatility. The difficulties might come at the wrong time and we don't want to be pulling money during a down market. Perhaps that money was exposed 30% to the equity markets and 70% to fixed-income markets. That would create a high probability that the portfolio would have positive performance over the 10-year timeframe.

Now we're left with $3,750,000 that we know we do not need for at least 10 years. Maybe we can get comfortable with the idea that that money could fluctuate up and down in price. Volatility would not be a great cause for concern because we know we won't tap into that bucket of money for 10 years. Under that circumstance, maybe there is a comfort level with having that money invested 70% in equities and 30% invested in fixed-income instruments.

Instead of pooling the money into one account (which may have happened while you accumulated it) when it's time to start utilizing your wealth, we highly recommend segregating your assets into at least three categories. You should segregate into what you need short-term, what you need in the mid-term, and what you plan to preserve for the long-term. That planning helps combat a lot of the emotional and psychological feelings that come along with volatility.

Tax planning is also a crucial component when figuring out your number. It's not just what your business is worth today, it's what your business would be worth today after taxes. The government is your partner, and unfortunately, they change their mind quite frequently about how much of your company they own.

This means you need to take a look at short-term tax strategies and what's on the horizon for long-term tax planning. If your company is worth $10 million today and capital gain tax rates are 20% this year but going to 30% next year, you need the value to grow by $1.35 million just to get the same after-tax value. This is why tax planning is so critical. Tax rates change often, so you need to be kept abreast of current practices and changes.

The fourth and final area of wealth, leaving a legacy, can be tied to a wide variety of estate tax planning opportunities. There are dozens of ways that are commonly used to avoid estate taxes if you feel comfortable that you have achieved financial security for your own lifetime. You can put in place ways to pass money on efficiently to your children, your grandchildren, charities of your choice, or others.

As of 2024, the federal estate tax threshold for married couples is $24.12 million. So, while you may not have a taxable estate this year, you might in the future based on your own asset accumulation or as a result of changes in tax law.

A lot of people feel like estate planning is an event. They had wills drawn up. They created testamentary trusts. They have a medical power of attorney or healthcare proxy. They have the financial power of an attorney. However, estate planning is not an event. It's not completed when you sign the documents. Estate planning is a process. When you start utilizing your wealth, your estate plans become all the more important. Understanding how transfers to your beneficiaries during your lifetime could impact you and your long-term financial security, both positively and negatively, needs to be evaluated regularly.

To summarize, in order to derive your number, you have to have an understanding of how much you're spending now, how much you plan to spend in retirement, what assets you have now, what you should expect from social security, pensions, or other sources, and how much money you're going to need to utilize from your own accumulated assets on an ongoing basis. While there is no magic formula, what's most commonly used is 25 times your annual need for cash flow. That will put you in the ballpark and then you will need to start evaluating your own personal circumstances.

Questions to Consider

- In what ways might you ease your transition from moving out of the wealth creation phase and into wealth utilization?

_____

_____

- Which of the 15 risk factors described are you most concerned about, and what might you do to thwart them?

_____

_____

- Could a "bucketing" approach to investing help you with your personal planning?

_____

_____

- Is it time to revisit your estate plan?

_____

_____

Chapter 4

WHAT AM I GOING TO DO WITH MYSELF?

"The grand essentials of happiness are: something to do, something to love, and something to hope for."

— ALLAN K. CHALMERS

This is one of the main reasons owners fail to plan. They have no idea what they'll be doing if they're not showing up at their company. People look at an empty calendar and think, "Oh, this must be what death is like." It is important to remember previous transitions. Think back to how you may have felt when moving from childhood to adolescence or from being a full-time student to becoming a worker. Do you remember moving out of your parents' home into your own place? What about getting married, becoming a parent, becoming an owner of a business? Change is difficult for most people to adapt to, but generally, when they look at their pasts and evaluate the change, they see it as positive.

Owners must start thinking and planning for how they're going to spend their time. Some people plan to stare at the ocean; kick back in the Caribbean with a book on the beach and a drink with an umbrella! Realistically, how long can you do that? I know—you'll also work on your handicap. But how many rounds of golf can you really play, and how long are you going to want to play?

We coach our clients to create an ideal week, create an ideal month, and look at an ideal year. Start by establishing a pattern for what you want to do during a typical day. Take a look at 10 different areas of life, in no particular order, and start working to establish goals in each of these areas.

1. Physical health activities and exercise
2. Intellectual stimulation
3. Recreation and creativity
4. Activities with your spouse or partner
5. Activities with family
6. Social connections
7. Residency
8. Spirituality and faith
9. Income-producing work
10. Volunteering and philanthropy

Oftentimes in early retirement, people tend to focus on one area over others and later in retirement perhaps they evolve and spend more time doing other things. But, the goal is to have a plan and to understand what you're going to do.

- What are you going to do before breakfast?
- What are you going to do for breakfast?
- What are you going to do between breakfast and lunch?
- What are you going to do for lunch?
- What are you going to do after lunch?
- What are you going to do for dinner?
- What are you going to do after dinner?

When you start looking at these 10 areas of life and evaluate the different things you'd like to accomplish in each, you can start charting them out into where the most ideal place would be to accomplish these individual goals. Retirement may not seem like a dark abyss anymore.

Maybe you like to exercise in the morning. Maybe you like to meditate in the evening. Maybe you prefer to have lunch with friends or to pick your grandkids up from school. Once you start planning out your week and saying, "This would be a fun week for me" and "This is actually something I look forward to," you'll start to escape the mental hurdles and the mental fear that's created when thinking about leaving your business.

The bottom line is, if you're not going to have something that's more fun, exciting, and rewarding to move into, then why make a change? Maintain your ownership. You should still have a plan for how to maintain your ownership while making sure that the business can succeed when the time comes that you no longer can, or want, to show up at the office.

Questions to Consider

- Which past life transitions created the most uncertainty for you? Looking back, do you think the change was positive or negative?

  _____

  _____

- What would your ideal day, week, and month look like if you no longer owned or operated your company?

  _____

  _____

- How will you maintain a sense of purpose and fulfillment without the daily structure of work?

  _____

  _____

Chapter 5

HOW WILL A TRANSFER OR SALE AFFECT MY FAMILY?

"Whenever you have truth it must be given with love, or the message and the messenger will be rejected."

— M.K. Gandhi

Many business owners can't even imagine the complexity that lies behind transferring their business and the impact that it can have on their loved ones. Many times there are no family members in a business and even still, the mere thought of getting this business out of mom or dad's hands and putting it into the hands of a stranger can wreak havoc on families. It's important to prepare, listen, and talk with family members about their thoughts about a transfer.

When we speak with owners who have family in their company and family outside the company, they think that the biggest hurdle is going to be treating family members equally. The reality, in our experience, is that open conversations lead to productive solutions. Owners need the courage and confidence to bring up these issues, often with the help of professional facilitators like Freedom Family Office, to get all parties thinking, and to find ways to address problems.

The reason that family issues have become so prominent during a transition of ownership is because the change highlights two different systems of thinking that we have in approaching business and family.

In a business system, we're focused on performance, finances, change, accountability, our marketplace, and being a stakeholder. In the family system, we're focused on communication, values, personalities, and camaraderie. These two systems are divergent in many areas.

A lot of business-owner families, especially those held by baby boomers, have one parent focused on the business system and one parent focused on the family system. Second and third generations become concerned that when both of those parents are operating exclusively in the family system, there will be new challenges.

If the family system has had a greater influence than the business system, then you're often going to have problems with the underperformance and accountability of family members within that business. You might have cultural issues in the business of nepotism. Exit planning helps to address these issues before they become destructive.

Conversely, if the business system controls the family, there might be a lot of resentment built up. This can be caused by members that either don't want to participate in the business, or are doing so reluctantly, or from those that don't participate in the business and feel like an outsider. Many families have an identity that is tied to their business and their ownership. Families want balance. They want the business to operate like a business and the family to operate like a family, but it's not that easy. 70% of family businesses fail to successfully transition ownership or wealth to their second generation. 90% fail to make it to the third generation and 98% fail to transition the business or their wealth to the fourth generation. That's where the proverb "shirtsleeves to shirtsleeves in three generations" comes from.

It's the same in Asia. They use the phrase rice paddy to rice paddy. In Holland, they use clogs to clog. This is a worldwide phenomenon. And there has been a lot of research in this area that tells us exactly why there is only a 2% success rate of wealth transfers.

Sixty percent of the reasons for failure relate to a lack of trust or communication. This is something that's almost always avoidable. 25% of these failures relate to inadequately prepared heirs. Again, some education, preparation, and expertise could fix this problem. So we know 85% of these failures might be preventable.

What's more amazing is that only 3% of failures relate to poor tax planning or poor estate planning. The professionals are doing an excellent job of preserving wealth. It's the families themselves that are unwilling or unable to communicate and prepare their heirs.

One of the worst practices is fostering a code of silence among the family in which people don't talk about issues. For instance, the issue of a son who doesn't produce at work, but still makes $200,000 a year and has the title of President or a daughter-in-law who is divisive and tearing her husband away from his father because she wants things one way at work and the father wants them another. Nobody is supposed to talk about these issues. These families forget about them and pretend they don't exist.

Those are precisely the issues that create problems with wealth transfer. They are bombs just waiting to explode. What we do is facilitate family meetings to get the issues on the table, break the code of silence, and strategically address ways that families can start tackling the distrust and concerns that they have for one another. This works well and it's much easier than it seems in 80% of cases.

One thing we encourage wealthy families to consider is hosting dedicated family gatherings, and not just Thanksgiving dinner. We're talking about beautiful retreats at wonderful places where families can not only connect and spend quality time together, but they can also have meetings and discuss issues in an open, caring way.

In Rich Beyond Money, we discuss the importance of helping include family in all of your experiences. Not only do you need to plan about the future with your family, looking for ways to get meaningful memories, while also realizing some of the thoughts and feelings they may have along the way. You may notice that a family member, like a child or an in-law, is upset about the business, but have you taken the time to ask? They may simply wish to have a chance to learn the business to receive your mentorship or worry they will miss out on that time with you. It is hard to know until you have sat down and discussed it with them.

It also provides a forum to inform new people in the family; a method to introduce them to the way the family does things. It helps promote a family culture. We also encourage seventh-generation thinking in which clients plan out a hundred years. How do we want this family to act and look a hundred years from now?

If you develop this mindset amongst your children and your grandchildren, it can persist. Some families have done this successfully. Unfortunately, it's only 2% who sustain this for four generations.

We have to take a healthy, balanced approach, which is not solely focused on money. It requires focus on the intellectual capital, the human capital, and the spiritual capital in addition to financial capital. Luckily, there are experts to help you. The worst way to try and manage these situations is alone. Incredibly sensitive issues benefit from an outside facilitator, someone who can set the tone, avoid lecturing, be independent, share their own insights about the family, and bring experience to the table to make the time planning together productive.

How Will a Transfer or Sale Affect My Family?

Questions to Consider

- With whom should you start talking and listening about the impact of a transfer on yourself and your family?

- Would a professional facilitator help create more productive family discussions?

- How might your "business system" conflict with your "family system"?

CHAPTER 6:

BUILDING THE TRANSITION TEAM

"I not only use all the brains that I have, but all that I can borrow."

— WOODROW WILSON

Are you ready to start putting together your exit planning team? It is critical to realize early on how many people might actually get involved in this process. It may become overwhelming to think about, because each of these experts might charge you on an hourly basis or a fixed fee, and the fees may seem daunting. Repeatedly, however, the investment in professional advice proves to provide a wonderful return on investment, especially as it relates to value enhancements for your business and tax planning that can be done on both a personal and corporate level. In many cases, we have created 20% to 40% increases in the net amount an owner receives by putting together a comprehensive, well thought out exit plan.

Let's talk specifically about each of the advisors that make up a transaction team. Without a doubt, you, as the owner of the company, are the most critical piece to the puzzle. Your involvement of time, effort, and a commitment of capital will lead the process and drive all the decisions. Your leadership will reign supreme over this project.

What owners experience through the planning process is often different from the day-to-day role of the CEO. There are two distinctions worth noting. First, the majority of the team we will describe below are professionals, and as such, get compensated for their expertise. If they do not fit in with the team, your style, or your objectives, they can be replaced without the same business challenges you face when terminating someone who works at the company. Second, the work is strategic. There should be virtually no firefighting, which, while you may be an expert at resolving, is often a draining experience. Strategy, on the other hand, tends to be energizing.

You may choose to include other shareholders, family members, or management team members on your transition team. These individuals should be selected carefully. While all shareholders should be informed about the process, and their needs considered as part of an exit plan, you may not want their influence or opinion to shape the details of the plan.

For example, one 80% owner wanted to liquidate his interest, but the 20% shareholder wanted to remain involved in the company. That shaped the exit strategy they selected. However, the 20% owner wanted to invest in growth, while the 80% owner was looking to take "chips off the table." If they were both participating in the exit planning process in a detailed way, there would be conflict over "grow then exit" vs. "exit then grow."

The same is often true for family members. While one child may work in the business and have a reason to advocate certain changes, another may be in a different field and see the business in a totally different light. While you should consider all viewpoints of the stakeholders throughout the planning process, the active participants should be kept to those who will support you in achieving your ultimate goals.

In general, your external resources will include your exit planner, accounting firm, corporate law firm, personal estate planning attorney, financial advisor, and insurance advisor. Since this book is about exit planning, let us describe the exit planner's role first. Exit planners typically become the quarterback of your team. In our firm, we call ourselves Chief Transition Architects. Exit planners have various experiences and education, and most come from either law, accounting, or investment banking, so they may fill one of the roles further described below, in addition to their exit planner moniker.

Our goal is to help owners bring in the correct advisors at the right time in the right order to streamline the process and make sure we are effectively tackling each issue one by one.

The exit planner's role typically starts with an assessment of the existing business structure, the existing goals of the owner, and the objectives that the owner wants to meet from a personal, family, business, and financial standpoint. Once the basics have been identified, the exit planner will start to build out a sequential process to map out how to accomplish your goals.

A common goal we uncover is that business owners need better metrics to monitor the performance of their business. They also need to increase the volume of service that they get from their accounting firm. As an example, many companies that are planning to exit to a third party for the highest price want to have audited financial statements, so that buyers who do their due diligence have financial statements upon which they can rely.

Having audited financial statements, even if they're not required by your current banking facilities or any investors, often generates a worthwhile return on investment, so it's important to understand how the accounting firm that you use now could provide you with that service.

Therefore, the accounting firm that has been managing the production of financial statements and the tax preparation for business returns (and typically personal returns for the owners) becomes a critical player in the exit planning process.

Of course, the tax aspects of a transaction are variables that can significantly impact the money that gets into your pocket, so your tax advisor needs to have expertise in asset structuring and tax planning. From an asset-structuring standpoint, we typically advise owners to segregate various asset pools into separate entities to protect themselves from certain liabilities.

In a construction company, for example, you might have equipment owned by one company, employees owned by another company, and management in a separate entity. By segregating these entities, and moving assets into different pools, you can protect yourself from certain liabilities while you are operating the company.

Similarly, when it comes time to do a transaction, you may be able to allocate the purchase price to different entities having different tax benefits, to both the buyer and to you as the seller. Asset structuring needs to be done at least a year before a transaction in order to benefit from long-term capital gain tax treatment. This is not something that can be done at the last minute.

For estate planning attorneys, their involvement tends to come into play early and often. For families that have created significant wealth in their company—wealth that provides more than sufficient value for the owner's generation to live comfortably—it becomes important to look at the estate planning opportunities a transaction provides. We will discuss common estate planning strategies such as GRATs and FLPs in Chapter 11.

Transaction attorneys are obviously a critical part of the transaction team as well. They will be the ones responsible for drafting purchase and sale agreements, negotiating various legal aspects of your agreement, and ensuring that due diligence goes smoothly and problems can be resolved.

Our most common recommendation to owners is to have your transaction attorney perform a due diligence audit or "mock due diligence" exercise. Due diligence tends to be the downfall of most transactions for two reasons.

First, owners are unaware of the amount of time and energy due diligence consumes for their management team and themselves personally. In addition, it often raises issues that were unknown at the start. Certain things like board resolutions, minutes to meetings, approvals for various projects that were done over time, etc. need to be addressed and cleaned up before a transaction so that you can avoid the surprises that get uncovered later on.

Having mock due diligence completed before entertaining a transfer puts you in an advantageous position. It will allow you to negotiate multiple deals simultaneously because your information is on hand and ready to go. This often requires the use of a secure data room where information and files are kept and prospective buyers can access that information on their own, in real-time, with permissions that you've granted to them.

Completing mock due diligence before negotiating a transaction eliminates the very real-time pressure faced by companies that are not prepared in advance. Your management team will also not get disrupted by deal inquiries while they are working on the important task of keeping the business growing and profitable while you negotiate a transaction.

The second aspect transaction attorneys often advise owners about are contract terms and negotiation opportunities. The contracts that you will have as part of your agreement are voluminous and complex. When you are at the heart of getting a deal done, you may not be in the right state of mind to evaluate each of the contract terms.

In most cases, owners do not actually read the entirety of the contract before they sign it. They look at their attorney and say, "Is this what you want it to be?" and when the attorney nods their head, they sign the agreement. In our experience, it is helpful to understand ahead of time what it is you might be signing, what it is that gets negotiated, and how each negotiation position might impact you.

The most popular agreement involving significant and broad negotiations is an employment agreement with the owner. Most owners become employed by the buyer for some agreed upon time for an agreed upon amount of compensation. This compensation varies widely from "reasonable replacement compensation" to significant portions of the total value of the company, called "earn-outs" that represent payments made based on the performance of the company.

In many cases, the earn-out is 25% to 50% of the total deal value. It's important to understand how these issues might get negotiated, and the impact it might have on the total value you could receive from your company. If your earn-out is part of your compensation, it will likely be taxed as ordinary income (and deducted by the company). On the other hand, your earn-out may be part of your transaction, in which case you may take advantage of lower long-term capital gain tax rates (and the buyer does not get an immediate deduction).

The transaction attorney will be able to walk you through each of the particulars ahead of time so that you understand when you're negotiating with buyers, what the different nuances between deals might be.

On the financial side, obviously having a great understanding of your current financial picture before a transaction, and the impact of the liquidity from a transaction, are of utmost importance. We will discuss this later in Chapters 10 and 12. Suffice it to say having a trusted advisor on the financial side is of critical importance.

The last type of consultant we mentioned is the insurance advisor. Insurance is an incredibly useful product for many varied reasons. In planning a transaction we often find life insurance becomes a key component of advanced planning for a transfer between family members, or even amongst the management team.

There are a variety of reasons for this. The most important is that premiums are often tax deductible. Subsequently, policies can be transferred to a different owner and the death benefit, when payable, can avoid income taxation and often estate taxation. It's a powerful tool that requires great expertise to implement in a sophisticated planning atmosphere.

Oftentimes we also recommend owners have a business coach, therapist, or clergy member that is available to them to discuss some of the emotional issues that go along with a transition of ownership. It is critical to realize that this transition is a significant life event. Beyond the financial aspects, there are significant emotional and social changes that coincide with the departure of the executive office. Being sure you are effectively prepared and coached to embrace your next chapter of life when you're no longer the leader of an enterprise, often means the difference between success and failure.

Questions to Consider

- Do you have an existing relationship with someone qualified to serve as your exit planner?

_____

_____

- What existing experts/advisors do you work with that you want to help with your exit plans?

_____

_____

- Would you like to protect your assets from creditors and enhance your ability to sell various assets while maintaining others?

_____

_____

- How much would a mock due diligence process cost you and what is the possible value it could create?

_____

_____

CHAPTER 7

CHOOSING AN EXIT STRATEGY

"The greatest enemy of knowledge is not the ignorance of knowledge, but the illusion of it."

— STEPHEN HAWKING

If you include an IPO, there are eight typical exit channels available for owners to exit their private companies. These eight exit channel strategies are divided between internal transfers and external transfers. Each offers a different amount of total value for the seller. A thorough examination of the value, benefits, tax implications, and overall desired outcome should be undertaken during the planning process so that the most beneficial exit strategy is chosen. An overview of six of the exit channels is presented below as recapitalizations and co-owner transfers are excluded.

Internal Transfers: Family Transfers

For small businesses, the most common transfer happens by default and is not the consequence of planning. Transfers to family often happen as a result of the death of the owner. The ownership of a company or membership interest transfers to the estate of the deceased. That estate is then distributed based on the terms of the will.

Often this leaves family members as owners of a company for which they have no experience running or interest in operating. Family transfers after the death of an owner erode value quickly and often result in the business closing or liquidating.

That being said, many families choose to transfer ownership from one generation to another; from parents to children or from siblings to cousins, nieces, and nephews. Family transfers often have the following significant benefits:

- The owner has total control over the transaction.
- The transaction can often be tax efficient.
- The terms of the transaction can be creatively designed.

Family transfers have a high failure rate, however. There are many risks among family transfers that don't exist with other types of transfers when it comes to the payment of the purchase price.

We recently heard of a father who transferred his business to his son after they had worked together for 25 years. Although the business was worth $15 million, the son had agreed to pay the father $5 million upfront and $5 million would be paid over time. The future obligation was not recorded as any type of indebtedness against the business.

The son, against the advice of the father, quickly started construction on a new facility that required the company to incur significant amounts of new debt. Unfortunately, the business failed as a result of the challenges faced by the son's expansion plans. Almost immediately after the closing, the son could not pay his father and the father walked away from the remaining $5 million he was owed.

The son, now without a job and bankrupt, had a strained relationship with his parents and also with his sister. The father had promised her the future payment stream of $5 million since he gave the son a "discount" on purchasing the business and wanted to treat his daughter equally. Now, as a result of her brother's actions, her "early inheritance" disappeared.

The main financial downside of a family transfer is that owners often receive less value than what might be paid by a third party at the highest price in a competitive auction. This type of transfer is also often the most complex because, beyond the quantitative issues, there are often many qualitative issues. These may vary widely, but common examples are motivation, knowledge, and dedication by the new family member-owner. Also, the issue of equality among the owner's children—some of whom may work for the business and others that may not—becomes one that needs to be addressed if maintaining family harmony is important. Therefore, when a family transfer is the desired result for an owner, exit planning is of utmost importance.

Management Team Transfers

The second type of transfer, which is also an internal transfer, is a sale to a management team. Commonly, management can operate the company, but it does not have capital sufficient to acquire the company. Like family transfers, owners often take less in the purchase price from their management team than they might otherwise receive from a third party. The risks of a management transfer are similar to those of a family transfer when it comes to the receipt of payment of value in the future.

Employee Stock Ownership Plan

The third type of transfer, the last type of internal transfer, is an employee stock ownership plan or ESOP. ESOPs are used by companies that have an ardent desire to share ownership with all employees in the company and not just management. Many ESOP transactions are motivated by the tax aspects of an ESOP buyer.

The intention of this book is not to cover the specifics of any one type of transaction, and therefore won't describe the details of ESOP transactions here. There are potential tax benefits that accompany an ESOP, however. Sellers of a company to an ESOP can, in certain circumstances, defer capital gains tax, possibly forever, and the ESOP, as a buyer, will receive certain tax deductions and tax protections because it is a qualified plan, i.e., a retirement plan that will benefit employees now and in the future.

External Transfers: Financial Buyer—Private Equity Transaction

Three other types of exit strategies involve outside buyers. The first is a private equity transaction. Private equity firms have continued to grow in popularity since the mid-1980s, now accounting for a sizable portion of mergers and acquisitions globally, driven by factors such as the increased costs and complexity of maintaining a publicly traded company. For many companies where an Initial Public Offering (IPO) would have made sense in the past, private equity firms are now better suited to be acquirers so that the costs and complexity of an IPO can be avoided. With the impending tidal wave of businesses that will be for sale, private equity firms will remain and increase the number of companies they acquire.

The purpose of a private equity firm is to take capital from individual investors or institutional investors, when a return on that capital is not needed in a short time frame, unlike investors in fixed-income instruments or often publicly traded securities.

Private equity funds have, as their main objective, the utilization of capital from investors to acquire companies. Often, experts within the private equity firm also advise companies on how to grow their businesses and provide them with the supporting capital to perform acquisitions and implement expansion plans.

One of the common traits of private equity transactions is referred to as "two bites at the apple." In the first bite, owners generally sell a majority interest to the private equity firm but remain owners of a minority interest, and also maintain operating control and operating leadership within the entity. The private equity firm's capital that goes to the owner helps secure the owner's personal financial future. In addition, the private equity firm provides the owner with the resources that may be required to implement a more aggressive growth strategy. Often, the private equity firm infuses additional funding into the company to pursue such plans.

The second bite at the apple happens after the private equity firm has maintained its ownership for a specific period, generally from 3 to 10 years. During this period, the firm has ample opportunity to grow the company and increase the value of the company.

When the minority owner and the private equity firm sell the company at the highest price in the future, the idea is that the owner should receive equal or more value for their minority interest than they did upon selling the majority portion of the company originally.

Private equity transactions tend to be most attractive to owners who would like to stay in the business. These owners often have confidence in their growth strategy, but may lack the resources to fund those plans, or prefer not to take those risks with their company. Private equity firms are often seen as the best solution in that scenario.

Strategic Acquisition

The next type of exit strategy is a strategic acquisition, meaning a company that would benefit from having access to the seller's business. The sought after advantage may be the seller's supply chain, their customer list, or any individual or collective component of the company.

Strategic acquirers tend to be either vertical or horizontal. A vertical acquisition means the selling company is a supplier, customer, or direct competitor. Horizontal acquisition is when other companies seek to enter a new market in which the seller has a presence. Strategic buyers often pay more for companies than private equity firms. This relates primarily to the synergies that strategic buyers anticipate.

Synergies are critical to identify so that they can help influence price. If your accounting department can be eliminated and those functions managed by the acquirer's existing personnel, that cost savings will influence the price a buyer can pay.

It is important to note that all third-party sales (e.g., private equity and strategic buyers) tend to pay more than internal transfers.

Initial Public Offering

The last exit strategy is an initial public offering or IPO. IPOs are quite uncommon among middle-market companies. However, many strategic acquirers are publicly traded companies and they will provide stock in their company in exchange for the seller's business interest. So, while an IPO may not be the exit strategy a seller anticipates, it may be that the seller will exchange ownership to acquire a public company's stock. One of the significant benefits of an IPO is often a higher valuation because of the liquidity or potential liquidity that exists at publicly traded companies.

How to Choose an Exit Strategy

We would like to talk about the valuation considerations and their impact on choosing your exit strategy. Each of the six exit strategies described above produces a business value that may differ from one strategy to the next. It may seem odd that a company can be worth different things to different people because most people believe the value is the value.

However, in a transaction, the value is determined by the buyer. As we described each of the six types of transactions, it can be noted that each has a different value potential. The private transfer strategies range from family transfers, which tend to have the lowest value, to management transfers, which have a slightly higher value, and finally, ESOPs, which have the highest. In external transactions, private equity buyers may pay more than the ESOPs. Strategic acquirers may pay more than a private equity firm, and an IPO may yield more value than a strategic buyer would pay.

To determine which exit strategy is appropriate for you, you have to consider the value you need to receive to achieve financial security when exiting your company. Additionally, you may have goals in mind for the legacy you leave. If your preference is to sell your company for the highest price to a third party, it is important to have a valuation completed that indicates an approximate amount of value.

Similarly, if your plan is for an internal transfer, whether it be to family, management, or through an ESOP, a valuation with that in mind is critical as well. Once you have determined if this value would be sufficient to support you in reaching your goals, you can move on to the next planning stage. If, however, you discover that the value you might receive under your preferred transaction is insufficient to meet your financial goals, you should consider enhancing your enterprise value through a variety of metrics.

Another key point in choosing an exit strategy is tax considerations. Each transfer has its own set of tax implications. Specifically, internal transfers can be designed to be more tax efficient, because of the control that sellers have in negotiating with internal buyers.

External buyers will not provide the same control to the seller and rather will control the acquisition themselves. This can have a significant impact on taxes, and it is important to seek professional advice on the impact each exit strategy would have on you regarding taxes.

It is important to take the time to plan the exit from your business. As you can see, there is much to be considered in each exit strategy. To choose the most favorable exit strategy to meet your current and future needs, each must be examined thoroughly with expert advice and input. Your quality of life and your legacy will benefit greatly from advanced planning.

The Best Metric to Measure

Your company's valuation or sales price is obviously an important number and accordingly receives most of the attention, but this metric is deceptive. The actual value realized by an owner is never the price or valuation; it is the accumulation of the price, structure, terms, and the corresponding tax impact. The Owner's Net Proceeds calculation considers all these value elements and delivers the amount an owner actually takes home.

The Owner's Net Proceeds Formula:

	Cash Valuation or Offer Price
Plus/Minus	Value of any assets or liabilities not included
Plus	Net present value of any seller financing (e.g., note, earn-outs)
Minus	Transaction cost and expenses (e.g., legal, banker commissions)
Minus	Company income tax
Minus	Personal income tax
Equals	Owner's net proceeds

The owner's net proceeds calculation should be the key financial metric for a business owner. By centering analysis and decisions on an Owner's Net Proceeds, owners can correctly evaluate and compare all their options. Plus, by focusing on this metric, owners can increase their net proceeds by proactively planning and managing each of the components.

Example Case

To illustrate that valuations or actual offers can be deceptive and why the Owner's Net Proceeds metric should be the key financial metric, we have created an oversimplified but practical example. The example assumes the underlying company is a C corporation.

Assumptions

Exit Channel	ESOP	Management	Strategic Buyer 1	Strategic Buyer 2
Valuation / Offer Price	$8.00M	$9.00M	$10.00M	$12.00M

Choosing an Exit Strategy

Asset or Stock Purchase	Stock	Stock	Asset	Asset
Seller Financing	$3.00M note at 7%— 10-year term	Estimated earn out $3.00M—5 years	N/A	Estimated earn out $3.00M—3 years
Financial Terms	All assets and liabilities	All assets and liabilities	Includes only operating assets and liabilities	Includes only operating assets and liabilities

Owner's Net Proceeds Calculation

Exit Channel	**ESOP**	**Management**	**Strategic Buyer 1**	**Strategic Buyer 2**
Cash at Closing	$5.00	$6.00	$10.00	$9.00
Net Present Value of Seller Financing	$2.87	$2.40	N/A	$2.58
Liquidation of Assets and Liabilities Not Included	N/A	N/A	$(0.50)	$(0.50)
Transaction Costs and Expenses	$(0.01)	$(0.01)	$(0.50)	$(0.60)
Company Tax	N/A	N/A	$(1.43)	$(2.07)
Individual Tax	$(1.60)	$(1.80)	$(1.61)	$(1.87)
Owner's Net Proceeds	$6.26	$6.59	$5.96	$6.54

In viewing the valuations/offer prices, the highest offer is 50% greater than the lowest offer but after considering the deal structure, terms, and the corresponding tax impact using the Owner's Net Proceeds formula, the variance is in a much tighter range of only 10% greater than the lowest net proceeds amount.

Owners need the right financial framework to evaluate their options, but the financial aspect isn't the sole consideration by most owners when planning and preparing for their exit. The above Exit Channel and Owner's Net Proceeds exercise is a useful tool that can unlock viable options that enable owners to accomplish all their goals.

There is a vast amount of complexity to any individual owner's analysis, so we encourage owners to seek qualified and unbiased guidance by working with an exit planner, CPA, or other advisor knowledgeable of the exit channel parameters and performing these calculations.

Questions to Consider

- Would you prefer an internal or an external transfer?

- When is the best time to tell your family about your preferred exit path?

- Think about your own company's culture and employee morale. How do you think an ESOP would impact these factors?

- Does the value you might receive under your preferred transfer strategy generate assets/income to achieve financial security?

Chapter 8

FIVE ESSENTIAL AREAS TO PREPARE FOR TRANSITION

"Where there is no vision, there is no hope."

— GEORGE WASHINGTON CARVER

Once you have decided that you're ready to make the transition from business owner to business seller, there are several specific things you need to consider. To prepare for the transition, a great deal of pre-planning and legwork needs to take place. There are five areas of a transition that should be taken into account, and each has several factors that should be examined. These areas are accounting, legal, financial, family and personal.

Accounting

The first category is accounting, and three main components in this area come into play: financial statements, key performance indicators, and personal expenses. First, when it comes to financial statements, you can self-prepare them or have a CPA firm compile, review, or audit them. In any case, a party interested in buying the business will do their own examination of financial statements.

Self-prepared statements, no matter what their state, will require the most in-depth examination by a potential buyer. This examination takes time, of course, which can prolong the period between signing a letter of intent and closing the sale. Delays during this time rarely benefit sellers and typically help buyers since they obtain more leverage as time moves on and sellers have more time, effort, and money invested in the deal process.

Having records compiled by a CPA firm may take less time to examine, but still requires a substantial effort on the part of potential buyers. Similarly, reviewed financial statements provide another layer of comfort for buyers in their analysis of financial data. This may reduce the time a buyer spends verifying the information compared to self-prepared financials.

An audit requires an accounting firm to invest the time and effort needed to verify the information provided by your company is accurate. Most outside buyers would prefer audited financial statements because it requires less time and expense on their part to make certain of your company's financial status. Therefore, evaluating the cost of having audited financial statements and weighing the benefits vs. cost is a critical step in preparing for a transition.

If your company maintains a significant amount of inventory, having statements audited will be even more important and valuable. If your records aren't audited, a buyer is going to want to perform their own audit of inventory, and that is going to take time and disrupt your business. If you have a regular audit, the auditors will come out to conduct an on-site review of your own inventory count and verify that the inventory that you list on your balance sheet is accurate. Potential buyers are going to have high confidence in your records with such an audit. Buyers are likely still going to do their own examination of your records, but with a current audit, they will not have to begin from nothing, saving you time during negotiations.

Choosing to have your financials audited, generally for 2 or 3 years before a transaction, does require an additional expense. In our experience, we would recommend auditing your financial statements if your earnings before interest, taxes, depreciation, and amortization (referred to as EBITDA) are over $1 million and you have substantial inventory. We would also recommend having audited financial statements for all companies with EBITDA over $2 million. The cost of an audit varies widely based on geography, company size, the complexity of your financial statements, and your choice of auditor. It always makes sense to ask your existing CPA firm what they would charge and to check with 2 to 4 additional CPA firms to understand competing options.

The second component of accounting preparation is to create and monitor "key performance indicators" or KPIs. KPIs can be financial ratios or management metrics, such as your sales cycle or your gross margin. You may have KPIs for each department within your company, as well as for your company overall. It is important to have some way to measure the success of particular activities or goals. When you are negotiating your letter of intent and your final contracts, current financial information that is readily available can affect negotiations.

If you have 3 years' worth of historical KPIs compiled at the time of your sale, it is going to give potential buyers a good sense of the trajectory of your business. If the information that your KPIs reveal puts your business in a good light, you will be better able to negotiate from a position of strength. On the other hand, if your information shows deficient performance, it gives you a tool to point out any periods of derailment in your business history. For example, perhaps you've had health problems and have been out of the business recovering and so your business has taken a few steps back without your leadership. Even though it is not information you want to highlight to a potential buyer, it does show that you are aware of the issues and that you know what needs to be done to rectify the situation and move forward.

Further, KPI tracking is a great tool to monitor and discuss the health of your company and as a basis for reward management. By showing a buyer that your team is capable of setting and achieving increasing levels of performance, you will garner a higher value for your company.

Finally, personal expenses paid by the business, often called perquisites, enter into the picture when considering your preparation for a transition. Most business owners pay expenses that may not directly relate to their company's out-of-business funds. For example, a spouse's cell phone may not be used for business, yet 100% of the bill is paid for by the company. Similarly, the owner may deduct 100% of their car expenses, even though the car is used primarily for personal use. The same may be true for meals, entertainment, and vacations. An owner might attend a conference and have the family come along for vacation, yet deduct 100% of the expense on the company financial statements and tax returns.

These types of expenses become what the industry refers to as "add-backs" and are evaluated as part of the deal when selling your business. Potential buyers want to know what types of expenses that were deducted from income tax returns or financial statements are not anticipated to become obligations of the acquirer.

> Long-term financial planning has a big impact on financial well-being. A key part of this is finding the right personal CFO or financial advisor for you. Once word gets out that you are selling your business, people will offer all sorts of advice regarding what you should do with your money. When you have a trusted financial partner in place, you can ignore all that noise and be confident in your course of action.

It is a good idea to start tracking add-backs in order to evaluate the amount being spent and how it is being spent. This examination may not result in any changes being made to your current accounting practices. However, if you're considering selling your business, or think that may be an option in the future, it is wise to keep track of these types of expenses. Three years later, you may not remember if dinner was business or pleasure. Tracking these expenses on an ongoing basis gives you a much better sense of the amount to be "added back" when it is indeed time to sell your business.

Legal

In the legal category, two significant things to consider are mock due diligence and the legal clean-up process. Mock due diligence refers to the process of taking a look at all the documentation that a buyer will require, but starting that process before entering into any negotiations with buyers. A transaction attorney or skilled exit planner can assist with this incredibly detailed process. Buyers always will have a list of paperwork they want to see: articles of incorporation, board resolutions, consent agreements among shareholders, insurance policies, company vehicle list, assets, bills of sale, terms with vendors and customers, supply agreements, organizational charts, etc. This is certainly not an exhaustive list. A recent transaction required the production of 30,000 pages of documentation!

The time between signing a letter of intent with a buyer and when the contract is signed is called the due diligence period. While you are negotiating the final points of the sale, the buyer is evaluating all that information to find out as much as possible about your business. A buyer does not want to enter into a deal with a company that has skeletons in the closet. They examine every bit of information with an eye to that, and also for any points which may provide them with a rationale to lower the selling price. The critical component here is time. You want the time between the letter of intent and closing to be as short as possible. If you don't have any of this data compiled ahead of time, you will be scrambling to produce it in a timely fashion. It is not always easy to find a vendor agreement signed a decade ago.

The idea behind mock due diligence is to gather this information, store it in one place, and have it readily accessible. The list of documents that buyers want to see is not a secret; you and your planning team can determine what buyers will be looking for. One effective way to keep this information current and available is to store it in an online data room. There are services with which you can store these important business records, financial statements, and other documents online.

When needed, you can assign permission to an outsider who needs access to the information—an accountant, auditor, or potential buyer.

Completing a mock due diligence process enables you to negotiate multiple letters of intent by giving prospective buyers access to a plethora of information you feel comfortable disclosing (after your receipt of a non-disclosure and confidentiality agreement). You will be able to increase the number of people you negotiate with if you have an online data room because your information is readily available and will not require significant effort to produce to multiple interested parties. Planning for this time-consuming aspect of a sale can help you work out the best deal for your business.

The other outcome of mock due diligence is the clean-up process. As you sift through and compile the information that is needed for due diligence, you will come across things that were supposed to be completed, but never were. Essentially, you are double-checking your previous work and cleaning up anything that was overlooked. Your attorney and exit planner will develop a to-do list of items during mock due diligence. These are the things you want to take care of before negotiating a transaction. For example, you may be missing employment agreements, strategic agreements with customers, or supplier agreements. This is a chance to improve the quality and efficiency of your business at an opportune time. By making this investment before a transaction, you use your time more wisely. During the hectic period when you are trying to close the sale of the business, you want to stay focused on the business and negotiating and not run around trying to gather documentation.

Personal Finances

Another category to consider is the personal financial aspect of a transition. You have to know what you need to be financially secure and be confident that this transaction will fulfill your financial needs. Earlier in Chapter 3, we wrote about knowing your number. Having a plan goes beyond just knowing this number, however. You need a system in place, before the sale closes, to manage newfound liquidity.

Five Essential Areas to Prepare for Transition

Without a plan to manage finances after a sale, most business owners put their money under a mattress. Many owners are not skilled at investing outside of their company. The lack of post-sale planning derails all the arduous work that was put into the sale of the business and can set an owner back 2 or 3 years. Not only do they miss out on potential investment earnings for those years, but they may lose a chunk of their money due to poor planning.

Long-term financial planning has a significant impact on financial well-being. It is critical to have a financial plan in place and to have a high degree of confidence in the plan. Before your sale closes, you should know the sale proceeds that you anticipate keeping after accounting for taxes, fees, and other costs and what your planned cash flow is going to look like. Take the time to plan and put that money to work for you to achieve your financial goals for your post-ownership life.

A key part of this is finding the right personal CFO or financial advisor for you. Once word gets out that you are selling your business—be it from a formal announcement or word of mouth—people will offer all sorts of advice regarding what you should do with your money. When you have a trusted financial partner in place, you can ignore all that noise and be confident in your course of action.

There are some key components to look for when selecting an advisor to work with. First, it is important to have a personal connection: Do you relate to this person? Do you have a similar philosophy? Often, this becomes evident through conversations around your transition financially, emotionally, and socially. If the person you meet is not someone you have a desire to share your financial and family concerns with, it does not matter how qualified they are. Think of this "hire" as you would when choosing your business CFO or President. It is someone that you want to speak with often, and if you do not "like" the person, the relationship will fail.

Assuming you "click"—look at their education, experience, and expertise. Education relays what they have learned and any certifications they possess which indicate their commitment to excellence. As far as experience is concerned: Will you be their largest client? Their smallest? How many other clients do they serve? Have they helped other people sell their businesses?

As it relates to expertise: Do they have clients with similar demographics? How would they apply their education and experience to help you? Are they a generalist or a specialist? Do they handle taxes? Insurance? Estate planning? Investments?

The change from CEO to no longer owning the company is perhaps the most significant in someone's life. There are so many different things to be considered and factored into such a change. Many are financial. Some owners may be inclined toward bad spending habits or illogical purchases as a way to compensate for the shift in their role. A good financial advisor understands the impact of these decisions and can help you weigh the pros and cons.

We urge business owners to seek advisors who are not only competent in the quantitative (numbers) side of personal finance but also have a keen focus on the qualitative (social, personal, emotional) issues that owners will face during the transition. Getting exceptional rates of return is rarely the key driver in the happiness of an owner. In Chapter 12, we will have a more detailed explanation of how to navigate the world of financial advice.

Family

The fourth area to prepare is the family aspect of a transition. We discussed certain aspects of this earlier in Chapter 5. One of the best ways to prepare your family for a transition, whether they engage in the company or not, is to hold family meetings. Communication among family members is critical.

Recently, a father was selling his business in which none of his three children were involved. He became enthusiastic about creating a family foundation to give back to the community. He wanted the children to be involved in the foundation, but the children had always viewed the business as a fourth sibling, favored by the father. They were resistant to becoming involved because they did not want to compete with the new "sibling" the father wanted to bring into the family. Had he gathered his family to discuss ways they could all participate and benefit from this transaction, he likely would have garnered a different result.

> The ideal situation is that you exit your company standing up and move on to another phase in your life that provides you with more happiness and is more rewarding than being a business owner. That takes time and deliberation to figure out.

The sale of your business will impact some aspects of family life, whether it's a relationship with siblings, your spouse, your children, or grandchildren. The sooner you begin a dialogue about the transition, the more time you'll have to work on any issues that arise. Sometimes this can be done with just the family, but often it is recommended to have a professional facilitator assist with family meetings. A professional brings a wealth of knowledge to the table that can help ease family members into open dialogue.

Considering that you are reading this book, you should have a dialogue—even informally—with your family to broach the subject. You could start with something as simple as posing the question, "If I sold the company—how do you think that might impact you?" Most family members who are not part of the company see this as a non-threatening question. They likely will say it won't impact them at all—which is just fine. But you may be surprised by an answer, and that is where real value and opportunity can come into play. It will provide you with advanced notice of how your loved ones may react to your choices.

In our Bonus Chapter 14, we discuss hosting family gatherings and other concepts you may find valuable if you have created sufficient wealth to support multiple generations of your family.

Personal

Finally, we arrive at the personal aspects of a transition. As discussed in Chapter 4, in contemplating the sale of your business, you need to envision a post-transaction life that is going to be more exciting and rewarding than your life as an owner. If you're not excited about the life you're going to live after you exit your company, then it's probably not the right time to sell your business.

Some people love what they do and don't want to do anything else. They plan on working into their 80s and 90s—as long as possible; their exit strategy is to die at their desk. There's nothing wrong with that approach, as long as you take into account the advanced planning that is needed so that your family isn't burdened with an asset that is suddenly worthless once you're gone.

The ideal situation is that you exit your company standing up and moving on to another phase in your life that provides you with more happiness and is more rewarding than being a business owner. That takes time and deliberation to figure out. We encourage owners to make a focused effort to plan out their post-transaction life. Get as excited as you were when you first started your business. It's important to plan for the success of your life, just as you plan for the success of your sale.

These five aspects—accounting, legal, financial, family, and personal—should be taken into account as you prepare for your transition. There is immense value in employing the processes discussed above. Each area can help increase your transaction value, make it easier to complete the transaction or save time for you and your business. All are key factors as you work to sell your business and transition to your post ownership life.

Five Essential Areas to Prepare for Transition

Questions to Consider

- What steps will you take in each of the five areas discussed?

- Should you have audited financial statements for your company?

- Which five KPIs should you create and monitor that would measure your business's health?

- How will you track your "add backs" so you can be sure to get paid the highest price?

- What would you do with your sale proceeds to recreate your current income?

- Which qualities are most important to you in your search for an exit planner?

- When would you like to host a family meeting or family gathering?

CHAPTER 9

COMPANY MANAGEMENT THROUGH TRANSITION

"Press on. Nothing can take the place of perseverance. Talent will not. Nothing is more common than unsuccessful men with talent. Genius will not. Unrewarded genius is almost a proverb. Education will not. The world is full of educated derelicts. Persistence and determination alone are omnipotent. The slogan 'press on' has solved, and always will solve, the problems of the human race."

— CALVIN COOLIDGE

When you exit your company, you want to get the most out of your time spent planning. To maximize your efforts, you need your employees' help to prepare the business for the transition and then to make that transition a successful endeavor. While you negotiate a sale, you need to keep the ongoing management of the company in mind to ensure that everything is running smoothly. To that end, there are four important aspects to consider: discussions with management, employee incentives, your personal assistant, and avoiding seller's remorse.

> It is important not to wait until the last minute to have a conversation with your stakeholders, both internal and external. You don't want to spring a sale on your team the day after a letter of intent is signed.

Discussions With Management

You should be having ongoing discussions with your employees and management team regarding your transition. This can be a complicated process to start, but the sooner it is done, the more beneficial it is. A one-time conversation to describe your transition is not an effective way to communicate with staff, but neither is constant discussion. There should be recurring discussions, perhaps during your annual strategic planning or budgeting meeting, or on some other scheduled, regular basis.

The purpose of having these conversations sooner rather than later is to evaluate where your management team is in their level of responsibility and authority. Once that is established, the next step is to find ways to delegate responsibility from the owner to streamline the management of the company. Ideally, the owner is not tied to running every major aspect of the business. The goal is to have owners who have a role in their business because they enjoy it, or because they are the best salespeople or the best CFOs. Owners who participate in roles in which they are highly competent are more successful than those involved out of necessity.

The value of a business is enhanced if the owner is not required to run the business. You want to become dispensable. It's a good selling point if a buyer will only have to replace some specific functions as opposed to a series of executive functions once the owner has exited the company. The first step is identifying all of your responsibilities as the owner. Next, you need to create a plan to have your management team assume as many of these responsibilities as possible. Typically you will need to focus on the performance metrics and/or policies and procedures that you want in place before assigning decision-making responsibility and authority.

It is important not to wait until the last minute to have a conversation with your stakeholders, both internal and external. You don't want to spring a sale on your team the day after a letter of intent is signed. Your management team is going to be required to participate in the due diligence process, and if they are not aware of that before it starts, there are going to be delays and setbacks while you discuss the sale process and reasoning.

If you do wait until very late to talk to your employees, the discussion must be handled very delicately. At that point, employees are going to be wondering about job security and may be upset at the lack of information they have received up to that point. This is an area where owners can find themselves "held hostage" by employees who demand unreasonable closing bonuses because they are worried about what the sale means for their employment and compensation. Losing a key employee during negotiations can derail the process, creating delays and possibly causing a deal to fall apart.

Employee Incentives

There are several ways to avoid these problems: sign employee agreements, implement employee incentive programs, or create a phantom equity plan. Employee agreements should be signed with all employees in the company, not just key staff members. Agreements should reflect terms that are important to you as an owner. Often, there are non-compete clauses or confidentiality clauses included in these agreements. It may be hard to enforce, but it is better to have an agreement in place, even if it is difficult to enforce, rather than have no agreement at all.

One of the best practices, especially for owners who are strategically thinking about their exit plan, is an incentive-based compensation plan in which the management team is given incentives for attaining certain goals or targets which are usually based on the earnings of the company. This helps increase the value of the company because everyone is working toward the same goal: increasing earnings. These incentive plans are also a way to keep management teams on board during the transition period to help grow the business and ensure a smooth change of hands.

A third option, which is often added in conjunction with incentive-based compensation, is phantom equity. In this case, the employee is not going to actually receive ownership of the business. However, they will receive money based on a formula when the company is eventually sold. For example, your business might be valued at $20 million, and you agree to give your key executive 5% of the sale price in excess of $20 million, paid 6 months after closing. If the company sells for $30 million, it will get 5% of the extra $10 million in value. That would result in $500,000 for the employee (and $9,500,000 for the ownership group).

Your Personal Assistant/Secretary

Another essential staff member to consider is your secretary or personal assistant. If your company has been in business for a long time and you have had the same personal assistant for much of that time, it is important to recognize the responsibility of that person and their role in the transition of the business. During the exit planning process, you, as owner, are going to have more meetings with the planning team and prospective buyers, more phone calls with advisors, and perhaps even tours of the company. A personal assistant needs to be in the owner's confidence in order to manage delicate issues as they arise during the transition. The personal assistant needs to know the facts in order to be able to handle sensitive phone calls or answer questions from inquisitive employees.

Owners often decide to give incentives to their personal assistants as well. This isn't necessarily the same type of incentive that management or the sales team receives. Rather, this is a post-transaction bonus opportunity so that the personal assistant will stay with the company through the transition. You don't want to lose a valuable assistant just months before your sale because of job security concerns. You want and need your assistant to stick with you through the transition period.

Often, this incentive is based on years of employment using a simple formula such as one week's pay for each year they have been with the company.

Another important thing to consider regarding this part of the transition is how many personal tasks your assistant handles for you. Perhaps the assistant picks up dry cleaning, schedules a pet sitter, or helps arrange travel for family members. As an owner selling your business, you need to recognize what your life will be like when you aren't the owner any longer and do not have this type of assistance. If it's feasible, an owner may consider hiring a personal assistant after the sale to continue as a household employee in order to help absorb the shock of the change the owner is experiencing. Having this support system in place can certainly help ease the transition into life after ownership.

> Making an exit plan isn't based just on age or the timing of retirement. Market timing, interest rates, economy and tax rates all factor into the optimum time to transition.
>
> You may think, "I'll sell when I am 66." Bue when that time arrives it may be a terrible time to see your business.
>
> You want to be prepared to take advantage when the timing is right.

Avoiding Seller's Remorse

The final aspect of managing the company through the transition is dealing with seller's remorse. This is a common problem with 75% of owners looking back on their transaction with dissatisfaction, regretting what they've done. Owners are often disappointed that they didn't have the foresight and planning to get the best price or terms to meet their financial goals. And then, after the transition, the life that they've moved on to is not as rewarding as the life they led as a business owner. After they've sold the business, had a vacation, spent time with family, and reconnected with friends, they miss the action and excitement of sales or problem-solving.

We hope that by reading this book and taking the steps to plan an exit strategy, seller's remorse can be avoided. Proper planning can and will resolve financial issues and concerns. More importantly, as part of the exit planning process, owners become actively engaged in the process of discovering how and why their lives will be more rewarding after the sale of their business.

To circumvent seller's remorse, however, an owner needs to have a realistic timeline to start the exit planning process. One year is the minimum and 3 years is probably the right amount of time for the majority of business owners. Five years, though, produces a less stressful and more rewarding experience for owners who aren't feeling pressure to sell.

Owners who aren't actively thinking of exiting their business are great exit planning candidates because they can think more strategically, without any time pressure. Someone who has just had a second heart attack, or has divorced and remarried someone younger that wants to travel and enjoy time together, may be under pressure to sell. They may not make the same decisions as an owner in his 40s who plans to run the business for another 20 years. Emotional factors can lead to rushed and regretful decisions. Planning, especially when you are not in a hurry to sell, gives you ample time to consider all options and outcomes and create the exit strategy that is right for you, your family, and your business.

Peter Christman, who calls himself the original exit planning coach, has a great frame of reference for the time it takes to create and implement an exit plan—"It takes one round of golf a month." So, if you devote the time of one round of golf, essentially 6 hours, toward exit planning every month over 3 years, you will be very well prepared. It's a consistent and repetitive commitment that will not overwhelm you but will give you time to succeed.

Making an exit plan isn't based just on age or the timing of retirement. Market timing, interest rates, economy, and tax rates all factor into the optimum time to transition. Similarly, if you plan an internal transfer to family or management, you want to be fairly certain they are mature, experienced, and ready to take on the responsibility. You may think, "I'll sell when I'm 66." But when that time arrives, it may be a terrible time to sell your business. There are a variety of factors that influence what the market is willing to pay for a particular company at any given time. You want to be prepared to take advantage when the timing is right. You can get your exit plan in place by a certain date and then you will be ready to make your transition when the other factors line up favorably.

It's important to make provisions for company management throughout the planning and transition phases. Selling your business can be a stressful time. Dealing with the loss of key employees in the middle of that process can cause many problems and setbacks. It is wise to give employees information as soon as possible and to reassure them, whether that's through continued conversations or incentive plans. As you transfer more responsibility from your shoulders to your management team, this is also a time of personal reflection and planning for your life after the transition. With the management of your company provided for, the transition period will run much more smoothly and efficiently.

Questions to Consider

- How will you approach starting discussions about exit planning with your management team?

- Will you offer an incentive-based compensation plan to retain your team through a transaction or transition?

- Why do you think 75% of owners regret their sale? How will you avoid the same fate?

- If you owned a stock like Google, would you plan to sell it when you reach a certain age, when it was worth a certain price, or would you want to sell it when you thought you could get the most for it given all the circumstances? How will you apply your answer to your own company stock?

- Are you willing to devote time to plan your sale now or would you prefer to wait and see what happens?

CHAPTER 10

DEVELOPING CLEAR MONEY INTENTIONS

"Wealth consists not in having great possessions, but in having few wants."

— EPICTETUS

It's important to contemplate how you plan to use your wealth and develop your own set of intentions. While your total assets may not change upon a transfer, having substantial liquid/investable wealth is quite different from the illiquid, concentrated wealth you had tied up in your business.

As an example, the business is likely paying some of your expenses such as car payments, cell phone bills, meals, or even travel. When you exit the business and can no longer deduct those expenses, you are faced with a sudden increase in your personal spending.

If you want to continue to maintain the same level of expenditure, you need to ensure that you will be utilizing an adequate amount of money. For the majority of owners, lifestyle spending will decrease post-transaction because there is some uncertainty regarding how long the money will last. For example, most owners find that relying on investment performance is not as comfortable as relying on the cash flow from their business.

For others, though, the sale of their business results in more cash flow than they have had in the past. An owner that was making $1 million per year may sell his business for $20 million. They now have a large pool of liquid assets they have not had to deal with before. While this can create a profound sense of financial security, it can also cause problems down the road as protection of the new-found liquidity becomes of critical importance.

Part of creating your exit plan is producing a concrete course of action for how you intend to use that wealth, whether that means saving for your own future financial needs or distributing money to some specific people or groups. There are five categories to consider when creating money intentions: children, grandchildren, siblings/parents, employees, and the community. Having a clear plan will also give you a clear, concrete response to any financial requests that you receive after your transaction.

When you consider the impact you want your wealth to have on others, you need to look at the people who are most important to you. Your children are affected by the sale of your business even if they are not directly involved in the business itself. If you are selling your business in your 70s or 80s, your children have likely achieved some degree of self-sufficiency. If they are relying on you for assistance, this exit is going to have even more of an impact on them. Either way, it is important to know how your sale will affect your children.

It's a clever idea to have a conversation with your children regarding your exit from the business and what your intentions are for your money and your family in order to avoid negative feelings about that. Silence is typically a product of thinking, "This is mine, I created it and I'll do what I want—it's no one else's business." This is what Josh thought. He and Marilyn, a couple in their 70s with three children in their 40s, sold their business for nearly $50 million. The children weren't involved in the business, but they were used to going on "business" trips with Mom and Dad. They all had received money multiple times when Josh would say "We had a good year, and so here's something for you."

Now that there was a sale, the kids were expecting a large gift. They figured, "They can't spend it all, so they should give it to us now, while our kids are young and it can make a difference to our lives." Josh had no plans to make gifts to the children. He didn't even think to discuss this with them before we met. We suspected that his children might have certain expectations, though they were unvoiced. Josh agreed to let us interview each of his kids separately, and we uncovered each of their desires and thoughts.

> Creating an open dialogue with your children ahead of time, no matter your intentions, is in the best interest of your family. Not only can these conversations put everyone on the same page, but they can also build closer ties.

Through a series of meetings and a family gathering, we were able to develop a plan that everyone in the family felt really excited about. It involved setting up a family bank and investment committee, where Josh did not give anything away but rather established a means for his children to learn alongside him and ask openly for financial assistance when they felt it was warranted.

Creating an open dialogue with your children ahead of time, no matter your intentions, is in the best interest of your family. Not only can these conversations put everyone on the same page, but they can also build closer ties. Money can often become a taboo subject with children, especially when they are young. There is also the fear that children will suddenly become unmotivated with a large financial gift. However, having these conversations is better for everyone involved and can produce incredibly positive outcomes.

Grandchildren are another consideration. In many cases, an owner's children have been raised modestly while the parents were working to build the company. Often, the second generation has become financially successful at a younger age than the parents. As a result, the grandchildren grow up having more than their parents did. Grandchildren may feel more entitled or privileged and have access to more activities, educational opportunities, and a lifestyle that may be costly to maintain.

This generational difference often creates a gap in your value systems. In this case, how do you want to impart the value of hard work or entrepreneurship to your grandchildren? You may see these values evolving differently among your grandchildren and the different families that they are a part of. Financial resources may also vary widely among grandchildren. For example, one family may be very financially successful, so the children get more vacations, go to summer camp, and have new cars. Another family may have a completely different lifestyle in which grandchildren have two working parents and spend vacations closer to home. Grandparents sometimes want to even out that disparity, which can become a source of conflict among children and other family members who view your method of distributing wealth as unfair. Having clear conversations with family members will help ensure that everyone understands what your intentions are and allows each member to voice their concerns.

Finally, when planning for a family involving your monetary intentions, your siblings and parents may come into consideration. Longevity has increased as medicine and healthcare have advanced. People selling their business may have parents who did not achieve the same level of success, and as a result, they may choose to assist their parents after, or even before, a sale.

Owners tend to be selling their business when their parents are in their 80s or 90s, a time when parents often need the most help not only financially, but physically. As a business owner, you and any siblings you have may possess different capacities to help your parents, which makes a conversation imperative.

One sibling, perhaps the business owner, may have the capacity to give the parents a monthly financial stipend to help with expenses. Other siblings may not have the financial means to do so, but there are other needs to take into consideration: transportation, upkeep of the home, bill paying, etc. It's productive to have a conversation with the family to divide the time and labor involved and to find a happy medium in which everyone can be involved in the life of their parents in a mutually beneficial way. Your exit planner can help facilitate this conversation to help the family consider and develop options, and to give everyone a chance to voice challenges and get answers.

After covering family in your money intentions, there are two other categories to consider: employees and your community. First, your employees have had a long tenure with you and they often have a sense of entitlement because of the time and effort they have put into the business. The best time to decide how you want to deal with them is before the transaction.

As an owner, you may choose not to share any of the proceeds of the sale with your employees. Alternatively, you may create a plan that rewards employees for their years of service. This may be especially appealing when you have a second- or third-generation family business with employees who have been in the company longer than some of the owners.

> As a business owner, you had ongoing cash flow to work with. When you sell your business, you're left with a large sum of money you never had access to or had a plan for before.
>
> Developing clear intentions for the use of that money is vital to ensuring your financial security.

No matter what you decide, you should create a plan that is in line with your family's expectations and values. Choosing not to share proceeds with employees is often the right choice for a variety of reasons, including your own financial security. In that case, however, you may want to find another way to reward employees to avoid hard feelings, resentment, and future problems for the company you worked so hard to build.

We recently helped a family that was selling their business after more than 50 years. They treated all their employees like family—decreasing owner compensation to avoid layoffs, accommodating those that needed temporary assistance—all the things you might read about in a success story for how to treat your team. At the time of their sale, they weren't sure how to handle the disparity between long-time workers who were unskilled labor versus their newer, younger, but more highly compensated executive team. In the end, we helped devise a formula that took a fixed bonus pool and allocated it based on earnings and tenure, with a heavy weight on tenure.

Finally, the local community has a significant impact on your transaction. If you've been a large employer in the community, sponsored Little League teams, or been active in civic associations, you will want to figure out a way to manage these relationships once you are no longer an owner. Perhaps you have been regularly active in the local Rotary club and you want to make a one-time donation or create a scholarship in honor of your sale and exit.

Giving to the community is not right for everyone. It depends on what your role within the community has been and what you intend it to be in the future. People and/or organizations will continue to ask you for money. You may not be the business owner any longer, but as a longtime sponsor, people will come to you to support their fundraisers and/or organizations based on your past involvement. Whether you plan to continue giving to the community or not, you need to have a clear intention for how you want to manage those situations. You should be confident and comfortable with your response.

As a business owner, you had ongoing cash flow to work with. When you sell your business, you're left with a considerable sum of money you never had access to or had to plan for before. Developing clear intentions for the use of that money is vital to ensuring your financial security. There are many options and considerations which make planning essential for your own peace of mind.

All of these considerations are heavily impacted by your personal financial plans. Exit planning as a discipline involves a lot of moving parts—personal, business, family, and financial—and tying each of these pieces together is both art and science.

Questions to Consider

- How do you want the financial success of your exit to impact those around you?

- What money intentions do you have for your children and/or grandchildren?

- How about your siblings or parents?

- What about your employees?

- Your community?

CHAPTER 11

BUILDING YOUR LEGACY

"We who lived in concentration camps can remember the men who walked throughout the huts comforting others, giving away their last piece of bread. They may have been few in number, but they offer sufficient proof that everything can be taken away from a man but one thing: the last of the human freedoms — to choose one's attitude in any given set of circumstances, to choose one's own way."

— VIKTOR FRANKL

Your legacy includes the story that people tell about you, your values, and how you pass those on to family and community, as well as your financial bequests. When you exit your company, you are leaving behind a whole story of your life. Part of your exit planning should focus on building and preserving your legacy —since your past will become a distant memory unless you preserve it. Your story involves manifesting a vision; and creating and growing a successful business. This is something that you should be proud of and will want to be remembered for.

Your actual story is the first aspect of your legacy that we recommend you focus on. Within a family, stories are told and passed down from generation to generation. We encourage our clients to share their stories not only verbally, but with written words as well. Dr. Judith Kolva, a professional who interviews families, compiles the story, and creates a memoir, says "The value of most things we purchase depreciates over time, but family stories only become more and more valuable as time goes on." Think of what you know about your family history. Are there pieces that you would have liked to have known? Think of how valuable it would be to have a written account from your great-great grandparents that shared the story of their early life, their successes, their daily life, and their family life.

As a successful entrepreneur, you are likely to value independence, hard work, and having a purpose. You've fought and won. You've lost and gotten back up. Those smaller details get lost in the retelling of a story over decades. There may be gaps of time in your family's future in which no one is an entrepreneur. This story of your life and your business success may be the thing that sparks the interest of a future family member, showing them what is possible to accomplish.

There are two ways to approach the writing of your story. For many owners, the easiest thing is to hire a professional. They will interview you, take notes or journals that you have, talk to other family members or colleagues, and do what is required to create a full picture of your life. They can take these accounts and craft a book for you, which can be printed, bound, and used as a wonderful family heirloom.

You can also do the writing yourself. If you have the time and inclination and do not want to spend the money on a professional, you can certainly author your own story. As a starting point, imagine the questions you might ask if you had the opportunity to talk to a great-grandparent you never knew. Where did you grow up and what was your life like as a child? How much education did you have? When did you get married? Start with a list of questions and then answer them for yourself.

You can write it out by hand/or even record your answers and have them transcribed and refined by an editor. What we have found, though, is that when stories are shared in a printed and bound book, they don't get thrown away. Histories live on, passed down through generations.

Company Management Through Transition

Your values are another important part of your story, and something you want to impart to your children and future generations. Hard work, independence, family, close ties to the community, and philanthropy are some values that you, as an entrepreneur, may possess. There are likely many others that you and your spouse wish to emphasize within your family.

One way to express these values is, again, in written form. Some people may prefer to have a professional help them determine, describe, and distribute a family mission statement or family value statement. Most families, however, do not have the time or resources to dedicate to such an undertaking. A family can create their own list of values using the tools available to accomplish such a task.

One of the main ways values are transferred is through family rituals. traditions that may take place during family holidays, special recipes treasured by the family, or "ways our family does X." When you were a business owner, your partner or spouse was probably responsible for coordinating and planning family holidays, vacations, and other get-togethers. Now, time that was dedicated to your business can be redirected to other events and functions of importance. You may take on a new role in these celebrations, or even take time to develop a new tradition within your family. One common experience we have seen is taking grandchildren for a "special" vacation without their parents or having them stay with you during school breaks as a way to build stronger bonds and share more of your values with them. Perhaps that is something you can explore when you are no longer focused on running your business. There are many ways that you can renew your role within your family while creating new rituals and sharing your values.

> Once you've exited your business, you'll need new challenges to go after. I suggest finding a way to use the skills you've spent your entire career building, to give back to causes that mean something to you.

Another common way to transfer family values through generations is via philanthropic activities. This could be significant giving or something that's everyday practice. A more firsthand approach is getting personally involved. If you, as an owner, participate in charitable activities, including children or grandchildren when possible, you are helping transfer the appreciation and rewards of helping and giving to others. It's also a wonderful way to share quality time with loved ones. In Chapter 14, we outline specific ways you can get started including your family in your philanthropy.

The monetary part of your legacy may come to mind first since most advisors take a quantitative approach when it comes to defining what you leave behind when you are no longer here. As we discussed in Chapter 10, you may choose to bestow gifts to your children or grandchildren or to make transfers as part of an estate planning process. You have several options in this area and each has different benefits and considerations.

There are many books written about tax-motivated estate planning, but we thought it would be appropriate to share a brief overview of some popular strategies. The first is a Zeroed Out GRAT (grantor retained annuity trust). This allows you, as the grantor, to make a contribution (in this case, stock in your company) into a trust. Over time, the trust repays you the value of the stock that was contributed to the trust plus interest. You decide the amount of the contribution and the government decides the minimum interest rate.

For example, a business owner decides to donate 10% of their company stock worth $1.5 million into a GRAT with a 10-year term. For simplicity, let us assume that over the next 10 years, the trust has to pay $102,000 back to the grantor yearly. After 10 years, the grantor received the initial donation of $1 million plus interest of $20,000.

The business might currently produce income and pay out a dividend. 10% of the total dividend would go into that GRAT, and then that dividend can be used to pay the grantor. If there are no dividends, or if they are insufficient to pay the $102,000, some of the stock can be used to pay back the grantor. Assuming the company pays dividends or grows its value over time (and therefore the stock increases in value) at the end of the 10 years, there will be something left in the trust. Whatever remains inside the trust is there for the beneficiaries and there is no transfer tax or gift tax associated with the transfer.

As a business owner, if you have the intention of giving money to beneficiaries at some point in time, but not at the present moment and/or if your business is likely to grow quickly and substantially and you want to protect that growth and pass it on estate and gift tax-free to your beneficiaries, GRATs can be excellent tools.

Another popular option is a Family Limited Partnership (FLP). A FLP isn't unlike a business partnership, except that family members are most often the partners. Owners contribute stock to the FLP, and then gift interests in the partnership to children, grandchildren, or charities. The value of the gift is always less than the pro-rata value of the ownership interest. In other words, if you contribute 10% of a company worth $10 million to the FLP (a pro-rata value of $1 million), then gift 99% of the interest in the FLP to your beneficiaries, the value of that gift for estate and gift tax purposes may be only $600,000—a 40% discount.

We would normally think 10% of a $10 million company is worth $1 million. Yet, the way the tax rules work, that 10% can be worth $600,000 if the beneficiaries have no control over what is going to happen with the company, the FLP, and especially if minority interests in the company cannot be readily and easily liquidated.

FLPs are great for owners who intend to exit their business soon. The business does not have to grow substantially to get value from using this structure for a gift. Even if the company doesn't grow, you are still basically saving money on gift or estate taxes by using an FLP. It is more likely, though, to see FLPs used for families with significant wealth, or those who intend to create significant wealth and have a proactive approach to planning.

The common and more simplistic transaction is an outright gift of stock to your company. An owner with two children may want to give 5% to each child, at which point each child owns a small portion of the company. This type of gift is a simpler approach than GRATs or FLPs, though a gift tax return must often be filed.

Both children now own 5% of the business and they will receive the benefits of that ownership. If the business has profits and makes distributions, both children will get their share of distributions. They will get tax reporting forms in order to report the income on their personal tax return. They also have rights as shareholders/members and if they choose to inspect the books and records of the company, they will be entitled to do so. A lot of owners want to gift the shares to their children but do not actually want to share the business information or decision-making with them. While this is a simple approach to giving to your children, it also gives your children, or other beneficiaries, more rights than they might otherwise receive under some of the other more complicated structures.

A fourth common way of gifting is actually selling stock to a beneficiary. You may choose to sell rather than gift stock for varied reasons, the primary reason being that you need the money. Your beneficiary may be involved in the business and you want to give them the company, but you need the money for your retirement, so you sell the shares. You may sell it to a beneficiary for less than you would sell it to an outside buyer. In this case, you will want to work with your accountant to make sure that the tax implications of such a sale are sufficiently accounted for. In terms of business operations, selling to a beneficiary is not much different than gifting the shares.

> Your financial giving is often the most complicated aspect of your overall legacy.
>
> It could hance the ongoing history of your family, inspiring and enabling your children or grandchildren to pursue their own dreams, which may include owning a business.

When evaluating any of these options for passing on a business interest to your children, grandchildren, or other beneficiaries, divorce is a serious consideration. With such high divorce rates, you need to think about the impact a divorce could have on your planning and financial intentions. GRATs and FLPs provide greater protection to keep assets within your bloodline or family for future generations. When gifting shares to a beneficiary who later divorces, in all probability there will be some disagreement about how much each spouse would be entitled to. Worse, if you sold the shares to your beneficiary and they then divorced, their spouse would share in the value of the business since the stock was purchased, and the business would be divided as if it were not a gift in the divorce settlement.

It is important to consider when and how you want to create a financial legacy for your family. Consideration should be given to whether you intend to make a gift or a transfer. The distinction between the two is significant for some owners when they plan out their financial intentions. A gift has the intention of improving someone's life. A transfer has the intention of avoiding taxes. If you as a business owner can answer the question about what your intention is, it will greatly inform your decision and planning process.

Your financial giving is often the most complicated aspect of your overall legacy. It is no more or less important than your story, however. In some cases, it could enhance the ongoing history of your family, inspiring and enabling your children or grandchildren to pursue their own dreams, which may include owning a business. Making a clear plan to pass on your own values and story along with your financial wealth will have an impact on your family for generations to come.

Questions to Consider

- Is it important to you to preserve your story? If so, how will you do it?

- What are your values?

- Are there any family rituals you want to create?

- How can you use philanthropic activities to share great experiences with your loved ones?

- Can you distinguish your estate plan from your wealth legacy goals?

- Do you intend to make gifts or transfers to your family?

Chapter 12

NAVIGATING THE WORLD OF FINANCIAL ADVICE

"The first key to wisdom is this – constant and frequent questioning... for by doubting we are led to question and by questioning we arrive at truth."

— Peter Abelard

When it comes to managing personal finances you have two obvious choices: hire a professional or handle it yourself. While that may appear to be a simple decision, there is much to consider before making a choice and moving forward. Do you want to oversee everything, including investing, on your own? Do you want complete control, but also have a way to ask questions, get advice and discuss ideas? Or, would you rather spend minimal time managing your money so that you can focus on other things? Careful consideration should go into these questions so that you are comfortable and confident in your course of action when your closing proceeds get deposited into your account.

Many owners feel that, though money is a complicated thing, they can manage it themselves. Before the sale of your business, you may have managed your personal finances. Post-transaction you likely feel that you're going to have more free time available to spend on such an undertaking. Some may question your choice, asking you if you would perform your own surgery, file your own taxes, or some other such thing. We don't see it in the same light, however. There are some investors and CEOs who want to have direct control of their money.

If you plan to collaborate with any advisors in some capacity, the most important thing to understand before working with anyone is how they are compensated. Investors have several options when looking for professional help, so we'll cover the main types of planners: fee-only financial planners, commission-only advisors, fee-based advisors, or hybrid advisors.

> It's important to have an idea of what advisor's motivations might be when they are offering advice and suggestions.
>
> You might take the advice of a commission-only advisor, who recommends an annuity product differently than if your fee-based advisor (who would not get a commission) did.
>
> Similarly, if your fee-based advisor is against your acquiring an annuity, perhaps they are motivated by the fact that you will reduce the assets they manage, and therefore the fees they earn from you.

Fee-Only Financial Planners

Fee-only financial planners are paid based on the time spent performing planning services for their clients. These services could be in many areas: insurance, estate planning, tax planning, cash flow management, budgeting, or asset allocation. Many fee-only planners have the Certified Financial Planner (CFP) or Certified Public Accountant with Personal Financial Specialist (PFS) designations. If they do not have these designations, they may be qualified based on experience in the financial planning industry in another capacity. It is important to note that there are no state or federal laws that regulate fee-only financial planners, so it is incumbent upon the investor to check credentials and references.

Many fee-only advisors only work with clients to create a plan (or update one) and then clients implement the plan on their own. This is a good option for those owners interested in managing their own finances. You receive professional advice, but at a fee that is either agreed upon in advance or based on the time invested. After meeting with the planner, you will either know what your fee is going to be or a general ballpark for the plan being created. You can then take that completed plan, based on what you've discussed with the planner, and implement the plan on your own.

Commission-Only Advisors

Another option to consider is commission-only advisors, which are often either insurance-related advisors, securities (stock/bond) brokers, or both. Insurance agents are affiliated with one insurance company, while insurance brokers have contracts with multiple companies. They primarily earn commissions on life insurance, disability insurance, long-term care insurance, and annuity contracts. Oftentimes, if you know you want a specific product, you can seek out an expert in that particular type of insurance. It is important to remember when dealing with a commission-only insurance advisor that they only earn money when you buy a product from them. All insurance agents are required to be licensed in the state(s) in which they do business, and each state has its own set of standards for what is required for licensure.

Securities brokers—often called "stock brokers" or "bond traders"—were the most popular form of commission-only advisors until recently. Brokers are required to have brokerage licenses, which vary based on the type of securities that can be traded as well as the products one can sell. Under the brokerage model, brokers only earn a commission when you implement their advice and make a trade (i.e., to buy or sell a stock or bond). While there are still many brokers, this business model has lost appeal to both advisors and investors. Historically, brokers had an ardent desire to encourage clients to trade so that they could make a living—but it may not have been in the best interests of the client. That said, some investors continue to seek out brokers so that they can access their brokerage firm resources and make trades based on their advice.

Fee-Based Advisors

Fee-based advisors charge fees based on the assets they oversee and/or manage. The fee-based model originated after certain brokerage clients felt they were not getting advice in their best interests. By charging a fee irrespective of activity, both the advisor and the client are motivated to grow the assets they manage.

Fee-based advisors often work for registered investment advisory (RIA) firms, large banks, or brokerage firms (for example Merrill Lynch, Morgan Stanley, Wells Fargo, UBS). RIA firms have taken a substantial market share position in the last decade. More than half of those investors with $1 million or more invest with RIA firms. While it's more common to work with a brokerage firm when you do not have significant assets, the number of brokers and brokerage firms has declined and RIA firms have emerged as the leaders of managing wealth for the affluent.

The primary reason for the growth of RIA firms over brokerage firms stems from the legal obligations of the advisors. Brokerage firms are required to adhere to a suitability standard. This means that any recommendation they make to a client must be suitable for that client. Suitable does not mean that it is necessarily the best option for that client. In many major brokerage firms there are cases where they have been sued by, or had enforcement action of some type by the Securities and Exchange Commission (SEC) because they were recommending products to their client base that may not have been suitable, or at the very least, were more advantageous for the banks than the clients.

Investors have become more aware of the suitability standards over the last few decades. They have come to recognize that they do not necessarily want what is suitable, they want what is best for their financial situation. That falls under another standard, the fiduciary standard. All RIA firms are required to comply with the fiduciary standard. This requires registered investment advisors to act in their client's best interest. If the best product for you pays them less money, that is the recommendation that will be made based on the advisor's commitment to a fiduciary standard.

Hybrid Advisors

Hybrid advisors earn a combination of fees and commissions. This model is the fastest growing since many commission-based advisors have seen the benefits of adding a fee-based model to their advisory business. In addition, some fee-based advisors have added commissions (primarily insurance commissions) to their business as well.

It becomes important for investors to understand why a hybrid advisor has chosen this business model. Many brokers are salespeople at heart and have now gotten the appropriate licensing so that they can also collect fee based revenue. Essentially, they have moved into the hybrid category. Just because they are collecting asset-based fees, however, does not mean that it is their primary area of expertise. Many only offer fee-based services as a means to earn more money and accommodate clients, even though they lack experience and expertise in the asset management business.

Why Compensation Matters

It's important to have an idea of what advisors' motivations might be when they are offering advice and suggestions about various products. You might take the advice of a commission-only advisor who recommends an annuity product differently than if your fee-based advisor (who would not get a commission) recommended an annuity product. In the same vein, if your fee-based advisor is against your acquiring an annuity, perhaps they are motivated by the fact that they will not get compensated for the product and that you will reduce the assets they have and therefore the fees they earn from you.

There are valid arguments from all sides as to which business model makes the most sense for investors, and clearly, there is no right answer.

For now, the migration of advisors is towards hybrid and fee-only models.

As a business owner going through the transfer process, it's important to figure out if you're working with the right team for your situation. When evaluating the commission-only, hybrid, or fee-based advisory models, there are several questions to ask. First, evaluate your current relationships. Are you working with insurance agents, brokers, or registered investment advisors? Is that the type of team you need now that you may have more money to manage and your financial outlook is more complex? It may be time to create new relationships rather than relying on what you had in place before your transfer.

The most common mistake owners make at this point in their financial planning is relying on a trust-based referral for a financial advisor. People take the referral without conducting independent due diligence and without understanding the dynamics of how the referral was made. A considerable number of referrals in the wealth management business are paid referrals. These should be disclosed to the client, but unfortunately, not all are. It is critical to ask the person making the referral if they will be paid if you work with their recommended person. It's important to know the answer because a paid referral might have a different standard than an unpaid referral. In other words, a paid referral may not be a personal recommendation based on prior experience.

There are a lot of different layers of expertise in money management. You may be referred to a commission-only salesperson who will offer you insurance products you really do not need. There may be a mismatch because the person making the referral isn't familiar with the information discussed thus far in the chapter so they cannot recommend someone who fits your greatest need. No matter the recommendation, it is important to research the referral.

Additionally, you need to make sure that the personality and philosophy of a potential advisor fit with your own. Do you like that person? Are they someone you would be comfortable sharing information beyond the financial, such as your personal situation and family issues or other things that may come up in a long-term relationship with a financial advisor?

Once you get past the personal aspects, you should examine quantitative aspects such as the advisor's education, work background, expertise, and clients. Do you fit into their client base? How many clients do they have? Some people would prefer to be the largest client and receive special treatment. Some would prefer to be a smaller client and work with someone who has clients they aspire to be like.

Taking the time to examine the information will give you a full picture of a potential advisor and what each can offer you. The person managing your friend's money, even if your friend is in an indistinguishable situation, may not be right for you. Just because you like some advisors personally does not mean they have the skills you need. Taking a referral without making an evaluation can be a costly mistake.

> If you do not want to work with a professional advisor on an ongoing basis, find a fee-only advisor (or a fee-based advisor that charges a planning fee) who can help you with some upfront planning. That way, you aren't totally on your own and you have a good map for managing your finances.

Breaking Down RIA Firms

Since most owners preparing for an exit will have over $1 million in liquid wealth to be managed and more than half of those investors are working with RIA firms, we want to provide a more detailed discussion of RIA firms. In the registered investment advisory world, there are four primary channels for managing wealth. The first are general RIA firms that manage investments for clients who may have $100,000 up to multiple millions of dollars. General RIA firms may or may not have a core focus on financial planning or investment management.

General firms tend to be created by a small group of entrepreneurial advisors who often "broke away" from a brokerage firm. In our experience, these firms are often the best solution for owners with $1 million or less of investable assets.

Another type of RIA firm is a wealth management firm. Most wealth management firms offer some component of estate planning, insurance planning, or tax planning along with investment management. The advisors often refer to themselves as wealth advisors or wealth management advisors. The use of "wealth" in their title is indicative of offering more services to clients and also striving to collaborate with clients who have several million dollars to invest. If you can work with a wealth management firm—typically they have minimum asset requirements of $2 million to $5 million—then often you get more service at the same cost than at a general firm.

A multi-family office is an RIA firm that works with many families but tends to have clients who invest $5 million or more. Our RIA firm, Freedom Family Offices, is a multi-family office. In this case, a client is relying on the firm for more than the four components of wealth management (insurance, estate planning, tax planning, and investment management). Some multi-family offices are focused on lifestyle and might offer personal security, travel arrangements, and services geared toward household employees such as drivers, cooks, nannies, or housekeeping. Others (like our firm) are more focused on intergenerational family planning. In this case, the firm may facilitate family meetings, and educate children about wealth and the responsibilities and opportunities created by wealth. The firm may also be a resource for younger generations while assisting with philanthropic activities and forming investment committees or family governance structures. A variety of other services may be offered as well, including bill paying, budgeting, and cash flow regulation.

A family office is another type of structure. This is a good fit for owners who have more of a do-it-yourself attitude and the knowledge and resources to create and run a family office. The founder, or wealth holder, hires their own team of full-time and/or part-time professionals. The owner typically manages the family finances, having all professionals report to that founder. These professionals are employees of the family office, which typically has a name and entity structure. This is generally an option for a family that has $100 million in assets and they are growing those assets. In this case, you would hire positions such as chief investment officer, chief financial officer, and investment analyst and pay them a salary out of the family's money.

With a stand-alone family office, you have employees rather than a relationship with a trusted advisor as you might have in a multi-family office or with a personal advisor. In the stand-alone family office, the owner has total control and can terminate employees. Employees could also leave. However, the family office would continue to run and hire new employees whereas a break with a personal advisor may cause an interruption in services.

The bottom line is that you need to know whether you want to manage your money by yourself or with a professional. If you do not want to collaborate with a professional advisor on an ongoing basis, find a fee only advisor (or a fee-based advisor that charges a planning fee) who can help you with some upfront planning. That way, you aren't totally on your own and you have a good map for managing your finances.

If you will be working with an advisor on an ongoing basis, it is wise to assess your current advisory team and reflect on their ability to serve you in the next stage of your life. It may be appropriate to research your options and interview potential advisors, even if you sense you will continue with your existing relationships. Take the time to find the advisor who is the best fit for your family, your type of wealth, and your financial intentions. This ensures that you will be confident in your choice of advisor.

Questions to Consider

- Would it be valuable to have a professional assist with managing your finances?

- Do you currently work with fee-only, commission-only, fee-based, or hybrid advisors?

- Is your current advisor the best advisor for your current situation? What about when you exit your company?

- Do you want your advisor to uphold the fiduciary standard or the suitability standard?

CHAPTER 13

WHERE DO I GO FROM HERE?

"There are risks and costs to action. But they are far less than the long-range risks of comfortable inaction."

— JOHN F. KENNEDY

It might seem confusing but there are a few different starting points. One is to undertake a "personal assessment" by starting to answer the questions—how is my life going to be more rewarding and fulfilling after a sale or a transfer? This can be done with your spouse, with an existing advisor/coach/mentor in your life, or with an exit planner that commonly works with owners to identify compelling reasons to exit a business, stay there forever, or anything in between.

Another starting point would be to simply look at a "financial assessment" to answer the question—how much money do I need to achieve financial security? You might want to sit with your accountant and financial advisor or start fresh with an exit advisor who is remarkably familiar with how to answer these questions quickly and efficiently.

A third option is simply evaluating your business. Answer the question—what's my business worth right now? Frequently valuations are completed by an existing CPA, an investment banker, or an exit advisor.

We hope this information has helped you understand the process and value of exit planning. At Freedom Family Offices we can do any or all of the things discussed in this book for owners of middle-market companies. You can find more information online at www.Freedom FamilyOffice.com or by calling 855-540-0400.

Please sign up for our e-newsletter so you can stay informed of articles, interviews, e-books, seminars, webinars, and conferences hosted by our company, Freedom Family Offices. To register, please visit us at www. FreedomFamilyOffice.com or email us at Hello@freedomfamilyoffice.com.

If you would like to share this book with a group of business owners, please contact us for a bulk discount.

We look forward to helping you.

ABOUT THE AUTHORS

Noah B. Rosenfarb, CPA/ABV/PFS

Noah B. Rosenfarb has dedicated his career to advising business owners on all things related to money. He is the Co-Founder and Chief Wealth Strategist at Freedom Family Office (www.FreedomFamily Office.com), where he serves as a Personal CFO and Holistic Wealth Coach. The firm provides middle-market business owners with guidance on how to successfully transition out of the management and/or ownership of their companies. Noah has served as an Exit Advocate for years, thoughtfully designing plans for owners to maximize the after-tax value of their businesses, achieve financial security, and maintain family harmony.

Noah's journey into wealth management began after graduating from Rutgers College with a degree in Accounting and a minor in Philosophy. He then became a Partner at a CPA firm that merged with Marcum, LLP. There, he helped business owners increase income, profits, cash flow, and the value of their companies through strategic business planning and performance-based compensation systems. His expertise in negotiating strategy and merger, acquisition, and divestiture activity was instrumental in the firm's growth from $2.5 million and 12 employees to $15 million and 70 employees over nine years.

Noah has successfully sold eight companies, taken one public, and completed over 50 real estate investments valued near $1 billion. His practical experience as an entrepreneur complements his technical expertise, offering high-performing families a balanced approach to financial advice. At Freedom Family Office, Noah leads a team of accountants, lawyers, and financial planners that coach seven-figure income and eight-figure net worth entrepreneurs on becoming Rich Beyond Money.

In addition to his professional accomplishments, Noah is enthusiastic about travel and has visited over 70 countries on five continents. He lives in Parkland, Florida, with his wife, Amanda, and their two children.

Noah is an expert witness and lecturer on topics such as business valuation, exit planning, personal productivity, investments, estate planning, and family office services. He is the author of numerous articles and e-books related to exit planning and maximizing prosperity. He co-hosts the Divestopedia Exit Strategy podcast, offering strategic insights for business owners planning their exits.

Noah can be reached at (561) 206-2126 or via email at noah@freedomfamilyoffice.com.

Peter Culver, JD

Peter Culver, JD, has over 25 years of experience in wealth management and is dedicated to helping entrepreneurs and their families achieve their financial and personal goals. As the Co-Founder and Chief Wealth Strategist at Freedom Family Office (www.FreedomFamilyOffice.com), he builds custom wealth plans for each client, starting with a detailed review of their current asset allocation, fees, and performance, and culminating in a tailored strategy that realizes their goals and values.

Peter's journey into wealth management began after graduating from Yale University (Cum Laude) and the University of Connecticut School of Law (With Honors). He practiced law in New York City and Connecticut for 12 years, representing trust companies and other financial institutions. This legal experience naturally transitioned into the wealth management field, where he served as Co-Founder and President of Sachem Trust in Greenwich, CT, and later as President of State Street Bank and Trust Company of CT. He then spent 14 years as Senior Wealth Director at BNY Mellon in New York City, where he was recognized as the #1 Client Advisor in the Wealth Management Group for 8 consecutive years and was consistently selected for the Platinum Circle and Chairman's Council.

Peter's passion lies in working directly with individuals and families, particularly entrepreneurs, to help them reach their personal and financial goals. He offers deep expertise in all facets of wealth management, including financial and estate planning, investments, insurance, family dynamics, and wealth transfer. Known for his ability to see the big picture and integrate all components into a cohesive plan, Peter is highly regarded by both clients and colleagues for his optimism, excellent listening skills, and responsiveness.

In addition to his professional accomplishments, Peter is actively involved in community service. He served on the Professional Advisory Committee of the Metropolitan Museum of Art and the Planned Giving Advisory Council of the Museum of Modern Art, and he held leadership positions with several other organizations, including Arts Horizons and Interfaith Housing Corporation. He is also a Board Member of the Long Wharf Theater and the Board of Finance in Guilford, CT, and has held various church leadership positions. Peter also enjoys coaching hockey and soccer.

Peter lives a fulfilling personal life, married with four children. When not spending time with his family, he enjoys running, swimming, biking, hiking, golf, gardening, reading, and solving crossword puzzles and mysteries. He resides in New York City and Avon, CT.

Peter can be reached at (917) 697-4156 or via email at peter@freedom familyoffice.com.

BONUS CHAPTERS

Chapter 14

CHANGING THE ODDS OF FAMILY WEALTH TRANSFERS

"Wealth is the slave of a wise man. The master of a fool."

— Lucius Annaeus Seneca

As of 2023, there are approximately 127,000 families in the United States with a net worth in excess of $25 million. If you fall into this metric, take heed of the research that explains why, for 98% of these families, their great-grandchildren will not see any of this wealth—it will be gone. This "shirtsleeves to shirtsleeves in three generations" phenomenon is primarily attributed to poor communication, a lack of trust among family members, and unprepared heirs.

Similar to how our focus on exit planning is designed to help you avoid the seller's remorse exhibited by 75% of business sellers, our post-sale wealth counseling is designed to help you thwart the issues leading to the disappearance of wealth. In serving as Personal CFO and Holistic Wealth Coach to families of affluence, we have first-hand experience implementing each of these strategies and have seen the difference they can make in creating positive engagement and lasting change.

Host Family Gatherings

If you have three or four generations in your family and don't already invite them to spend vacation time together, this is a great first step in building family identity and creating lasting memories. Family vacations may have often been spent at your vacation home, but we encourage clients to seek destinations that provide a combination of easy travel for all family members, opportunities for fun activities, and a relaxing atmosphere. Unfortunately for many families, the vacation home does not do all three of these things.

When hosting family gatherings, resist the urge to obligate your children and grandchildren to a structured regimen. Offer a schedule of things you will be doing/hosting. Provide advanced notice for where and when you will be eating meals, what activities you plan between mealtimes, and what evening activities you are organizing. As your tradition matures, many find it helpful to form committees to select the dates and location, to organize the schedule of activities, and to infuse common family meeting topics of family mission, vision, values, and governance.

> We encourage all our clients who are in a relationship to go through this process collaboratively. After doing this together, many couples realize that the "build, sell, set for life" plan they initially envisioned for their business was a misguided effort.

Family Philanthropy

There are great ways to foster a tradition of giving among your family members and also to build certain skill sets among your next generation. One of the easiest ways to implement a family giving program is to provide each of your family members with their own donor-advised fund (DAF). In simple terms, you make a donation to the DAF (and receive the benefit of the tax deduction), but your family gets to decide which organizations will receive donations. This is both simple and convenient.

Another strategy we recommend is to underwrite contest-style giving. Each child or grandchild presents to the family the charity they wish to support—their reasons why and the use of the donation. This can be done as an oral or written presentation (or both). After hearing all the options, family members vote on the most compelling gifts. Oftentimes, every presenter's organization is given a minimum gift, while two or three of the chosen organizations receive larger gifts. This strategy does a few things well—it gets your family together to talk about giving to others, provides an opportunity for younger generations to learn oral and written presentation skills in a comfortable environment, and everyone learns the methods of how others choose organizations.

A wonderful time to implement the "contest" is during a family gathering. Before leaving, make sure everyone knows the date and time when presentations will take place. You may choose to begin the tradition of having the eldest present first, with the youngest presenting last, or vice versa. Ask all family members to keep score of which charity they think is most deserving and have them submit their recommendations to you. At dinner during the vacation, announce the winners and be sure to have everyone start thinking about the charity they will want to represent next year.

Creating a Family Bank

Although this may sound formal and fancy, implementing a family bank structure can be quite simple to start. Ideally, everyone in the family will come to recognize that your wealth can be utilized to support and reward positive behavior—not as a means to avoid hard work or self-discipline. The family bank would commonly fund education expenses, business ventures, or opportunities to support family members' goals.

The main distinction between gifting and family banking is accountability. Generally, there is some type of application process (beyond a simple request) and a review process. We recommend that you involve outside advisors and/or family members from other branches of the family in the decision-making process. This is an obvious sign of creating an accountability culture in your family around requests for money. Commonly, there is also a repayment plan or objective so that the family bank can exist and perpetuate for future generations.

Investment Committee

Becoming an experienced investor is usually done through trial and error—and errors can be costly. By forming an investment committee, knowledge can be shared and transferred between generations in a supportive environment. More importantly, family members with deep knowledge within a specific arena can apply their skills to benefit the entire family. To form an investment committee requires two things—a pool of money or assets to be managed, and a group of people willing to take on the responsibility.

We often recommend that the asset pool be substantial enough to be taken seriously (no less than 10% of invested wealth) and that the matriarch and/or patriarch do not participate on the initial investment committee. Instead, one member of each branch of the family is asked to participate to get the process started (and having sons-in-law and daughters-in-law participate is a great practice). The family CFO/financial advisor and/or outside Chief Investment Officer/money manager should facilitate the meetings and design the agenda until a family member wants to take over. Having an investment committee work together with your advisors does a few very positive things. First off, it builds a relationship between two important groups of people in your life. Second, it allows you to witness the level of care, attention, and performance your family will dedicate to preserving and growing wealth. Based on the results, you may choose to increase the pool of assets the investment committee oversees, or you may determine that when you are no longer capable of managing the majority of your wealth yourself, your best course of action is to have paid professional advisors manage it for your family.

What Will You Implement?

By implementing these concepts, your family will have a much greater chance of preserving wealth and developing a healthy and positive attitude toward the role money can play in the lives of your children and future generations. Establish a goal for yourself to infuse one of these programs into your family and work with an advisor to make sure you are successful. Only good things will come from starting the process now.

Questions to Consider

- Do you care if the wealth you provide to your heirs is squandered?

_____

_____

- What are you willing to do to educate and motivate your family to become responsible stewards of wealth?

_____

_____

- Do you want to host a family gathering with a professional facilitator?

_____

_____

- Would having a family bank help you address requests for money more comfortably?

_____

_____

- What experience do your children have with investing? When would you like them to gain more experience?

_____

_____

Chapter 15

LESSONS LEARNED FROM BUYING AND SELLING COMPANIES

By Ron Mehta

"I've come to believe that all my past failures and frustrations were actually laying the foundation for the understandings that have created the new level of living I now enjoy."

— Tony Robbins

I came to the United States in 1970 as a graduate student after earning my bachelor's degree in chemical engineering at the Indian Institute of Technology—Bombay. I went on to get my master's degree in chemical engineering at the University of Connecticut. Following that, I worked toward a PhD in Material Science and Engineering at the University of Utah, but I did not complete it; instead, I got a master's degree in engineering administration.

After finishing my formal education, I worked in several engineering jobs with increasing managerial and executive responsibilities. In 1990, I left the corporate world and ventured out on my own making large plastic returnable water bottles. My overall success, though dotted with false steps, gave me interesting and solid insights into the process of planning for and selling a business.

Crystal Clear, Incorporated

My first venture into ownership was in 1990 when I started Crystal Clear, Incorporated, located in Hillside, New Jersey, a plastic blow molding company that manufactured large returnable water bottles. An incomplete marketing plan and flawed financial analysis meant that Crystal Clear did not take the local area by storm, namely the northeast corridor. Fortunately, the company had a unique, patented bottle design: a hexagonal bottle with a round top and bottom. This was developed over the first 6 months that the company was in business, via a trial and error process. When exported, the company was able to take full advantage of the honeycomb-like stacking capability which allowed us to fill a 40-foot sea shipping container with 19% more product.

As a result, the company developed significant international business. The unique bottle design attracted the attention of one of the largest resellers of water bottles in California, with that company ordering multiple container loads per week.

Another company in Modesto, California, Pure Systems, sought out a strategic partnership with Crystal Clear. Pure Systems made pure water machines and sold water through those machines at grocery stores. Together, our two companies built a $1 million plant in Modesto using real estate that the owner of Pure Systems already owned.

My new partner was 25 years older than me. He was not interested in taking risks, while I was very growth-oriented. We had a 50/50 joint venture which I discovered does not work well in most cases. Someone has to have authority to make a decision, and in retrospect, I learned that I should have initially insisted on majority control.

Another issue was in the workforce. My partner's daughter was the general manager. She was an excellent employee, but additional relatives employed by the company were not as hard working or interested in the health of the company. I had concerns about these relatives continuing to be employed by the company. Since I had no authority to terminate his family, they stayed with the company.

The final conflict came when a new investment was needed in order to expand further. My partner was not interested. He saw all the risks in the deal and, frankly, the upside would not have changed his life. Unfortunately, we weren't making money at that point. My partner decided if he could just get out of the personal guarantees he had provided to finance the purchase of equipment of about $800,000, he would consider relinquishing his interest to me.

To implement the expansion plans, I bought my partner out by paying for the real estate he had contributed to the business and I took on an additional loan plus all the personal guarantees — a huge risk. As part of the arrangement, Pure Systems signed a 5 year sales contract to continue to purchase the bottles.

In late 1994, after the manufacturing sites in Hillside, NJ, and Modesto, CA had been streamlined, the company secured a contract with Coca-Cola of Colombia. As a result, we became a major threat to the largest returnable bottle manufacturer in the world, Reid Plastics, Incorporated. Reid was a $40 million privately owned company with multiple plants in the United States and joint ventures in Canada, Mexico, and Israel.

Reid was expanding rapidly, fueled by a capital infusion from a private equity group, and they made me an offer I could not refuse. I saw Reid as a growth opportunity and in 1995 I merged my company with theirs. Reid paid me one-third of the price in cash, one-third in Reid stock (3.5% equity), and one-third in preferred stock with an 8% Payment In Kind (PIK) dividend. As a condition of the merger, I continued employment as the Vice-President of International Business and also was appointed a Director.

From 1995 to 1997, we rapidly grew by making six acquisitions and grew from $40 million to $220 million in sales. During these acquisitions, I noticed three common owner mistakes made when we approached the sellers. Unfortunately, these all applied to me as well. My goal of this testimonial is that you avoid the same fate.

First, nearly everyone we acquired did not have a competing offer— we approached them before they were marketing their company for sale. There is a saying that "one buyer is no buyer." Because we were not in a competitive buying situation, we were able to pay less than we would have if they had been prepared and sought out a buyer pool.

Second, most owners had no idea about what the due diligence process would look like and were unprepared for the process. They fumbled through it like chickens with their heads cut off. Their management teams had to spend the day running the company and the nights trying to gather information and reports for us. It was always incredibly stressful for the owners, their team, and their attorneys. We were able to use this to our advantage— always negotiating at the end of the process additional discounts or terms we were looking for.

Third, owners did not understand how the deal structure (asset deal vs. a stock deal) or purchase price allocations would impact their net proceeds—the amount of money that they actually put in their pockets. While their CPA could run the calculations for them, they were unprepared and not positioned to negotiate these aspects as we were applying pressure—"take our deal or we'll walk away"—thus, we were able to negotiate favorable terms for Reid.

After integrating our acquisitions, which was an integral part of our own strategic exit plan, the existing private equity group, the Reid owners and I sold the company to a larger private equity group at a scaled-up and rewarding EBITDA multiple. It was a fabulous financial return for all of us and an experience that taught me so much about mergers, acquisitions, divestitures, and how to run a valuable plastics company.

Plastic Industries, Incorporated

In 1998, after selling Reid and upon termination of my employment contract with Reid's new owner, I teamed up with a new partner. I met him when we both worked at Reid and he was the President. Together we purchased Plastic Industries, Incorporated, a small, barely profitable blow molder in California for $4 million. We each contributed $250,000 in equity and I contributed another $500,000 in debt capital along with co-guaranteeing a bank loan for the $3 million balance. Having learned from experience, I insisted that one of us had to own controlling interest.

Since he was going to be the Operating Partner on the ground in California, I graciously agreed to let him have 50.1% and I held the remaining 49.9% equity. To protect myself, I also constructed a detailed management agreement with the help of an excellent legal advisor and an outside accounting firm. Our detailed management agreement clearly outlined all governance items in minute detail, so that going forward we would not have any management issues. I did not want to make the same mistake twice.

> Although my team included very good U.S. advisors, I did not have a good Canadian tax advisor. To my dismay, I discovered that we were considered a foreign entity operating in Canada. My proceeds were impounded with 30% ultimately held back. After nearly a year, I was able to collect about half of what had been held back. If I had the proper tax advice up front, I would have avoided the headache and disappointing financial outcome.

Canam Plastics, Incorporated

6 months after the acquisition of Plastics Industries, while still barely profitable, we had the opportunity to start from nothing a blow molding company, Canam Plastics, Incorporated, in Brampton, Ontario, Canada. At that time, the Canadian dollar was very weak at approximately $1.4 CDN/$1 US which gave us a great advantage in terms of production cost. The opportunity was attractive because I envisioned our ability to be the lowest-cost producer in the northeast for blow-molded watering cans. We secured a 3-year "take or pay" contract with a large distributor of lawn and garden care products in New Jersey. I negotiated the purchase of the start-up facility with the help of an excellent legal

advisor and CPA. The investment required $1.1 million of cash, which I provided via a loan to the company.

We signed a 3-year contract with our customer and rapidly completed construction of the manufacturing plant in Canada. We made Canam Plastics a wholly-owned subsidiary of Plastic Industries. I then hired my former plant manager, who I met during my tenure at Reid, to run Canam. Canam started profitably producing millions of 1, 2, 3, and 5-gallon watering cans for a New Jersey supplier of home and garden products. The exports to the United States accounted for 95% of the company's sales.

After 18 months, Canam's management approached us, wanting to expand into an area in which I still had an active non-compete with Reid. They had a thoughtful and wise strategy and I did not want to hold them back. I sold my ownership to the Canam general manager and a Canadian investor for a significant return on my initial investment and signed a noncompete where I was prohibited from competing in Canada for 5 years.

Everything had gone very well with the creation and sale of Canam except for one item. Although my team included exceptionally good U.S. advisors, I did not have a good Canadian tax advisor. To my dismay, I discovered that we were considered a foreign entity operating in Canada. My proceeds were impounded with 30% ultimately held back. After nearly a year, I was able to collect about half of what had been held back. If I had the proper tax advice upfront, I would have avoided the headache and disappointing financial outcome.

Premium Molding, Incorporated

In 2001, I still owned Plastic Industries and it was running well without my day-to-day involvement. Somewhat bored, I began the search for another blow molding company. I put a $317 ad in The Plastic News stating that I was looking to acquire a company in Northeastern Pennsylvania or New Jersey. I received a reply from Premium Molding, Incorporated in Derry, Pennsylvania. It was 40 miles east of Pittsburgh, well outside the desired geography in my ad.

Where Do I Go From Here?

Through our discussions, I thought I could add value and I felt the price we agreed on was advantageous to me. I did not do extensive due diligence, no legal due diligence, or any investigation or review of human resources at the company but I did hire a CPA to do the financial due diligence and to review their records. All appeared to be in order. I invested $5.3 million for a 53% equity interest. The remaining 47% continued to be owned by the founder of the company, a man 14 years younger than me. The company was located in an antiquated facility at that time, 310 miles away from my home.

Until this point in time, I had operated companies with a highly diverse workforce, often with a majority of immigrants who valued their jobs. The workforce and culture in western Pennsylvania were a surprise. I did not do any research or check on the culture of the company or the area in which it was located. Premium Molding had a workforce that was almost entirely local, with little diversity. The plant was non-union, but compared to my previous ventures, the workforce came from a strong unionized background. There was heavy absenteeism, alcoholism, and illicit drug use. This was a problem I could have uncovered had I performed a more comprehensive due diligence.

The good news was the company had a stellar customer list and took immense pride in growing the customer base. Because of my optimism, in 2003, we took on significant debt to build a new plant 10 miles away in Latrobe. The new facility took us from an out-of-date 80,000-square-foot facility to a massive 217,000-square-foot facility. We purchased the underlying real estate and invested $2.5 million in new equipment to create a state-of-the-art facility.

At the same time we were building the plant, we purchased Diakon Molding, a run-down company with a long history in blow molding, including blow molding for extremely large parts. As part of the purchase, we acquired a fairly large facility in Reidsville, North Carolina. Shortly after, a customer that supplied Honda wanted to purchase our Diakon Molding facility so that they would be near Honda's plant in Alabama. We made a large return on our investment as a result, but unfortunately had to pour all the proceeds back into the Premium Molding expansion in Latrobe.

To make matters worse, in 2006 disaster struck in the form of sexual harassment claims involving my minority partner, dating back to before I had invested in the company. The partner was immediately forced to resign. That created a tremendous amount of upheaval in operations and the company lost momentum and production efficiency. The most recent recession hit in the first quarter of 2020 due to the COVID-19 pandemic, causing similar financial disruptions where many businesses had to secure additional investments due to banks freezing lines of credit. Premium Molding was then forced to move its relationship to the bank's restructuring group. In early 2009, I hired an investment banker to attempt to sell the company. It would have been a distress sale at that point, as no one wanted to purchase real estate and no one was willing to pay any amount close to what I had invested in the company. Finally, in the late third quarter of 2010, a private equity group out of Ohio chose to purchase the company, though the amount did not even cover the outstanding bank loans. To get out of my personal guarantees to the bank, I agreed to the sale and then settled with the bank for an additional $1.5 million to be paid over 2 years. Overall, my total investment of $8.3 million in Premium Molding was a complete loss.

It is said you learn more from failure than success. I don't know if that's true, but I learned a lot from my experience owning Premium Molding. My number one mistake was not evaluating the character of my minority partner or the partner staying on. I also failed in not performing the proper due diligence, specifically due diligence regarding the culture of the local area and the workforce. If you are not familiar with a target company's culture and workforce—get familiar. They can make or break you and it is important to know what you're walking into and working with.

Also, do not expand without ascertaining that there is going to be growth with profits. I thought our new facility's automated work process would decrease costs, but the reality was that the "old way" was not terrible. We ended up with growth—but without profits—and it destroyed the business. Additionally, if you are in manufacturing, steer away from investing in brick-and-mortar real estate. There are certainly value and tax motivations from "paying rent to yourself" but if you are focused on your core business, you should create enough value and profits to accomplish your financial goals. Finally, do not take risks so large that they can break your company apart. These were all lessons learned the hard way for me.

Back to Plastic Industries

Through all of this, Plastic Industries continued to grow primarily by growing with our customers. Our largest customer in 1998 made $1.5 million in sales and by 2011 they had grown to $13 million in sales. Along the way, we learned to develop and negotiate long-term sales contracts with key customers. Based on these agreements, we had the confidence to build multiple plants. Our original facility moved from Garden Grove, CA to a brand new facility in Corona, CA, and new plants were built in Fresno, CA, and Hebron, KY.

Finally, in 2011, we became motivated to sell the company because of personal health issues. My experience with selling companies gave me a great perspective to rely upon when planning my own exit. The company was doing well—making over 25% in EBITDA, which remains exceptional in the manufacturing sector.

After extensive review and interviewing of investment bankers, we found an excellent candidate who not only put together a tremendous book but at the same time also brought other people to the team such as estate planners and wealth advisors. Our team discussed estate planning laws, the tax outlook, our company performance, and our personal goals. Together we were able to review our personal, business, and financial goals so that we could make sure the exit fulfilled our goals and priorities.

Plastic Industries was an attractive business by design. We were growing with our customers and had long-term contracts with multiple customers. 80% of sales were tied up with customers who had 4- to 5-year supply contracts. This eliminated a lot of risk from the buyers' perspective—they had reliable cash flow into the future. In addition, approximately 95% of our workforce was reliable immigrant laborers who valued their jobs and served the company loyally.

Moreover, we owned no real estate; all our facilities were leased. Of course, we had to get the landlord to approve the reassignment of the lease to the new owners. The landlord became confident that the company wasn't going to fold and the buyers gained certainty the investment in property improvements would not be lost.

As a result of our proactive planning, we had set certain criteria that had to be met in order for us to sell the business. Our first condition was we would only entertain offers structured as a stock sale. Initially, we turned down a $31.5 million deal from a private equity group because they wanted to hold back $5 million in escrow and were also suggesting we take a note for part of the purchase price (i.e., lend them money to buy our stock). We knew we were not interested in any of this so, even though it was difficult, we were confident we understood the marketplace and turned down the offer. Eventually, the private equity group buyer came back and the offer was increased to $33 million with escrow cut back to only $2.5 million with no note—structured as an all-stock sale.

With over 22 years of experience that included 1) starting from scratch, 2) doing multiple company acquisitions and divestitures, and 3) managing, growing, and expanding businesses, I gained valuable insight and knowledge regarding exiting a plastics business. Here is a summary of the top things I learned along the way.

First, **once you decide that you want to sell your business, begin proactively planning your exit**. Planning five years ahead is recommended but if not feasible, at a minimum, three years will give you a decent time frame for getting everything organized. **Have your financial records audited**, or, at the very least, have them reviewed so that your financial statements and performance history are in order.

Once you are nearing an exit, **minimize your capital expenditures (CAPEX) in the final two years of ownership** so long as it does not have any negative impact on performance or sales. Buyers care about the CAPEX requirements. The loan or money that they secure for financing the deal is going to be based on the current cash flow of the company and the ongoing CAPEX of the company going forward. A great deal of capital investment can impede a potential buyer.

Develop a well thought out estate tax plan to manage the income you are going to receive in the sale. Do not just make general plans for the money, but **have specific intentions for that money**.

Settle your family and business affairs by **completing a "mock" seller due diligence process**. For example regarding family: if you have family members who are employees, cull any unproductive or problematic family members before the sale. They can negatively impact the sale of the business so you want to make sure that any issues are resolved before potential buyers begin their own due diligence process.

Remember that **timing is everything**. Be aware of what is happening in your business, in your planning, in the economy, and in the particular area where you operate. Get your plan in order and be ready to execute it when the timing is right to sell.

Strive for an all-stock sale. Often that will be difficult. If you are unable to get a buyer to purchase your stock, then understand what an equivalent asset sale price would need to be to net you the same amount in your pocket after taxes.

Limit your post-sale financing structure. In other words, do not leave any post-sale buyout such as a buyer note or an employment contract if you do not know the buyer to be trustworthy, or if you do not plan to remain involved in the business.

Finally, **build a great advisory team**. It takes more than a CPA and an attorney to collaborate with you to create a well thought out and complete exit plan. Look for an experienced certified exit planner who can help you create the strategy and build out your team. Most teams require an investment banker, wealth advisor, CPA, tax advisor, and a merger and acquisition attorney to help create the plan and cover all aspects of the sale along with assisting your post-sale with your wealth and estate planning.

Questions to Consider

- What mistakes might you be making if you don't have an exit plan?

- Are you planning to exit your business with the advice of experts or all on your own?

- Do you anticipate getting bored and then acquiring another business? If so, should you "love the one you're with"?

- How will you be ready when the time is right?

CHAPTER 16

53 WAYS TO MAKE YOUR BUSINESS MORE VALUABLE

This bonus chapter is a resource we often utilize in our practice. The purpose of this "workbook" is to maximize your company's value by viewing your business through the eyes of a prospective buyer. We created this tool by collaborating with numerous merger and acquisition (M&A) professionals who collectively have over 200 years of experience selling middle-market companies. We have distilled their insights into 53 crucial "value factors" buyers consider when determining the value of a company.

We have organized these 53 factors into six categories:

1. Business Operations
2. Financial
3. Legal/Regulatory
4. Industry/Market
5. Economic/M&A
6. Personal

In addition, we have created a scoring framework that will help you efficiently assess, prioritize, and implement changes at your company. We recommend you first read the contents, then go back to the beginning and enlist your management team in completing the scoring and questions. Ultimately, this can be incorporated into your company's ongoing strategic and business planning.

How to Use the Score Boxes

Score all 53 factors by first scoring the Potential Value Impact (A) and then scoring the Relevance (B) to your company. Then add the two numbers together and the result is your Value Enhancement Score for that factor.

	Potential Value Impact (A)	**Relevance (B)**	**Value Enhancement Score**
	1 lowest to 10 highest	1 lowest to 10 highest	(A) + (B)
Score	6	8	14

Your score estimate as to the Value Impact or Relevance should be based on an informed understanding of your company and your industry peers. Each factor should be approached from a buyer's viewpoint... what you would look for if you were doing an acquisition?

After you have scored all 53 factors, focus on the three highest Value Enhancement Scores. These are the factors that are most relevant and can provide the greatest value impact for your company. To get started implementing value changes, collaborate with your management team to create an action plan using the format provided in the workbook.

Action Items	Priority	Date	Who
1.			
2.			

How to Use the Workbook

We recommend you begin the workbook by first reading and understanding the importance of each factor and then answering the self-assessment questions associated with each factor.

Where Do I Go From Here?

Next, score all 53 factors by first scoring the Potential Value Impact (A) and then scoring the Relevance (B) to your company. Then add the two numbers together and the result is your Value Enhancement Score for that factor.

Your score estimate as to the Value Impact or Relevance should be based on an informed understanding of your company and your industry peers specific to each factor and for every factor it should be approached from a buyer's viewpoint ... what you would look for if you were doing an acquisition.

If you have questions regarding any of the factors or need help with scoring, we can provide you with a no-cost 15-minute consultation. Please call us at (855) 540-0400 or email support@freedomexit.com to schedule an appointment. In addition, if you would like a copy of this chapter to download, please ask the team!

1. Management Team

	Potential Value Impact (A)	Relevance (B)	Value Enhancement Score
	1 lowest to 10 highest	1 lowest to 10 highest	(A) + (B)
Score			
Business Operations Factors			

Reason for Importance: The management team is critical to the success of a business both during and after a transition. Buyers place significant value on a strong, experienced, and well-aligned management team because they are responsible for maintaining operations, driving growth, and ensuring the continued success of the company after a transition. A well-prepared management team can provide confidence to buyers that the business will remain stable and profitable after the current owner exits. Additionally, a cohesive management team can help facilitate a smoother transition, minimizing disruption and maintaining employee morale.

Where Do I Go From Here?

Self-Assessment of Your Company

1. Are the members of your management team capable of leading the company without your direct involvement?

_____

_____

2. Is there a clear succession plan in place for key leadership roles within your management team?

_____

_____

3. What incentives or retention strategies are in place to ensure the commitment of key management team members during and after the transition?

_____

_____

Action Items	Priority	Date	Who
1.			
2.			
3.			

2. Sales Team

	Potential Value Impact (A)	**Relevance (B)**	**Value Enhancement Score**
	1 lowest to 10 highest	1 lowest to 10 highest	(A) + (B)
Score			
Business Operations Factors			

Reason for Importance: The sales team of a company not only services existing customers but also has to find new customers. It's smaller companies, the sales staff is small, and often the function is performed by the owner(s). Relationships are established with a few good customers and this is usually enough to keep the company growing at a modest rate. Buyers, however, are normally interested in higher growth. Without an established sales team that has consistently found new customers and generated increasing sales, the buyer will consider the deficiency to be a substantial risk to the success of their investment. This is especially true if the owner is the salesperson for the company and is retiring from the company after a sale. On the other hand, a sales team with a history of success provides the buyer with a level of confidence that the business will continue to grow in the future.

Where Do I Go From Here?

Self-Assessment of Your Company

1. Which accounts are you the key salesperson in?

_____
_____

2. Does the company have a strong sales team with a record of new account growth?

_____
_____

3. Does the sales team collaborate and timely communicate opportunities and issues with management and other departments?

_____
_____

4. If the company utilizes sales reps, is the company's business a significant and profitable part of the reps' business?

_____
_____

Action Items	Priority	Date	Who
1.			
2.			
3.			

3. Information and Financial Systems

	Potential Value Impact (A)	**Relevance (B)**	**Value Enhancement Score**
	1 lowest to 10 highest	1 lowest to 10 highest	(A) + (B)
Score			
Business Operations Factors			

Reason for Importance: Information and accounting systems are important to buyers because they are the focal point for the collection and reporting of data needed to effectively run a business. The system should be integrated so that all the functions of the business are utilizing the same data and should have enough capacity so that a buyer will not have to invest additional dollars into upgrading or expanding the system for several years. To the extent that the software is customized, a strategic buyer will be concerned about integrating the system with his own computer system. In summary, buyers want the seller's computer system to work well on its own, integrate easily with their own system, and not require any additional investment in the first several years.

Where Do I Go From Here?

Self-Assessment of Your Company

1. Do the company's systems provide management with accurate, timely, and meaningful data and reports?

_____

_____

2. Is the system's capacity sufficient to meet the company's needs over the next several years or will it require an upgrade or replacement in the near term?

_____

_____

3. Does the company use a standard software package or does it operate proprietary software that was developed in-house?

_____

_____

Action Items	Priority	Date	Who
1.			
2.			
3.			

4. Location

Score	Potential Value Impact (A)	Relevance (B)	Value Enhancement Score
	1 lowest to 10 highest	1 lowest to 10 highest	(A) + (B)
Business Operations Factors			

Reason for Importance: Location is important to buyers because it can have an impact on costs, access, cost of living, and domicile desirability. If it is too remote, employees may not want to live at that location because the availability of qualified labor may be restricted. Shipment costs for both outgoing and incoming freight can be high and extra delivery time may be required for shipments. If the business is located in a high-cost area, employee wages, rental costs, and other operating costs can be higher than competitors creating a competitive disadvantage.

Where Do I Go From Here?

Self-Assessment of Your Company

1. Is the company location convenient to vendors and customers?

_____

_____

2. Are competitive transportation services available?

_____

_____

3. How does the cost of living in the local area compare to other areas?

_____

_____

4. Is skilled labor readily available at competitive costs?

_____

_____

Action Items	Priority	Date	Who
1.			
2.			
3.			

5. Efficient Organizational Structure

Score	Potential Value Impact (A)	Relevance (B)	Value Enhancement Score
	1 lowest to 10 highest	1 lowest to 10 highest	(A) + (B)

Business Operations Factors

Reason for Importance: Buyers seek an organizational structure that promotes open and timely communication regarding the company's affairs and the markets in which they operate. In addition, buyers seek an organizational structure that allows the company to efficiently and effectively implement initiatives to reduce risk and increase revenues and margins.

Where Do I Go From Here?

Self-Assessment of Your Company

1. Do you have an up-to-date organization chart?

_____

_____

2. Does the structure promote open and timely communication throughout the organization?

_____

_____

3. Have recent company initiatives or performance provided evidence that the organizational structure is sufficient or requires modification?

_____

_____

Action Items	Priority	Date	Who
1.			
2.			
3.			

6. Management Succession Plan in Place

	Potential Value Impact (A)	Relevance (B)	Value Enhancement Score
	1 lowest to 10 highest	1 lowest to 10 highest	(A) + (B)
Score			
Business Operations Factors			

Reason for Importance: Buyers prefer organizations that have development and management training initiatives in place. This protects in the event a manager leaves the company due to a sale or from some other event. In addition, management succession plans provide a buyer with the flexibility to reallocate resources where needed and promote a culture of growth and opportunity for the company's workforce.

Where Do I Go From Here?

Self-Assessment of Your Company

1. Do you have depth for each key employee or manager in case of their departure or would you have to recruit externally?

_____
_____

2. Does part of your management's assessment include identifying and grooming employees?

_____
_____

3. Do you offer employees education incentives?

_____
_____

4. Do you have an interim plan in case of the departure of any of your key employees?

_____
_____

Action Items	Priority	Date	Who
1.			
2.			
3.			

7. Management's Focus on Growth and Value Creation

	Potential Value Impact (A)	Relevance (B)	Value Enhancement Score
	1 lowest to 10 highest	1 lowest to 10 highest	(A) + (B)
Score			
Business Operations Factors			

Reason for Importance: Buyers achieve or exceed their expected rates of return typically by focusing on growth and shareholder value initiatives. Accordingly, they seek companies with a management culture that prioritizes this and is not absorbed in day-to-day management or constantly in a reactionary mode. Such a culture helps assure a buyer that the resources and structure are already in place which lowers a buyer's risk and also supports a higher growth and value forecast; correlating to a higher price for the seller. This is often evidenced by showing prior year business and/or strategic plans, and the realization of prior goals.

Where Do I Go From Here?

Self-Assessment of Your Company

1. How much of your management team's time is spent strategically planning?

_____

_____

2. Do you conduct offsite management retreats?

_____

_____

3. Would you classify your company as initiative-taking or reactive?

_____

_____

Action Items	Priority	Date	Who
1.			
2.			
3.			

8. Active and Visible in Community and Industry Affairs

	Potential Value Impact (A)	Relevance (B)	Value Enhancement Score
	1 lowest to 10 highest	1 lowest to 10 highest	(A) + (B)
Score			
Business Operations Factors			

Reason for Importance: A seller's management that is actively involved in community and industry affairs stays informed of the markets that affect a company and positions a company to plan and capitalize on opportunities proactively and strategically. In addition, the visibility of being involved can create company creditability, marketing, and networking opportunities.

Where Do I Go From Here?

Self-Assessment of Your Company

1. What organizations are you and your management members of?

_____

_____

2. Do you or any of your management team hold a leadership role with any industry association?

_____

_____

3. Does the company support and contribute time to any non-profit or charitable organization?

_____

_____

Action Items	Priority	Date	Who
1.			
2.			
3.			

9. Sale and Marketing Literature

Score	Potential Value Impact (A)	Relevance (B)	Value Enhancement Score
	1 lowest to 10 highest	1 lowest to 10 highest	(A) + (B)
Score			
Business Operations Factors			

Reason for Importance: A buyer's perception of how the market views a company is important and can be influenced by the company's sales and marketing literature. Accordingly, the company's sales and marketing materials should be up-to-date, attractive, and informative. More importantly, it should clearly articulate your marketing messages.

Where Do I Go From Here?

Self-Assessment of Your Company

1. Are the company's sales and marketing materials up-to-date, attractive, and informative?

_____

_____

2. Are materials available in both digital and hard copy formats?

_____

_____

3. Does the company have an online social media presence?

_____

_____

Action Items	Priority	Date	Who
1.			
2.			
3.			

10. Customer Relationships

	Potential Value Impact (A)	**Relevance (B)**	**Value Enhancement Score**
	1 lowest to 10 highest	1 lowest to 10 highest	(A) + (B)
Score			
Business Operations Factors			

Reason for Importance: Buyers want to determine their risk post-closing of losing customers due to an ownership change. Companies that have positive and long-standing customer relationships with multiple people within the company are preferred and reduce their risk versus customer relationships that rest solely or are dependent on the relationship of the exiting seller or certain employees of the seller.

Where Do I Go From Here?

Self-Assessment of Your Company

1. Does the company have positive and long-standing relationships with its customers or do customers turnover quickly?

_____

_____

2. Are the customer relationships with the company or are they dependent upon the owner(s) or certain key employees?

_____

_____

3. Will the owner or key employees who have customer relationships stay with the new owner?

_____

_____

Action Items	Priority	Date	Who
1.			
2.			
3.			

11. Vendor Concentration

	Potential Value Impact (A)	**Relevance (B)**	**Value Enhancement Score**
	1 lowest to 10 highest	1 lowest to 10 highest	(A) + (B)
Score			
Business Operations Factors			

Reason for Importance: Buyers favor companies that aren't dependent on any single vendor or group of vendors as this minimizes their leverage and ability to control cost, outages, and service levels. Buyers expect a company's raw materials and other inputs readily available from multiple sources at competitive prices.

Self-Assessment of Your Company

1. Is the company dependent on any single vendor or group of vendors?
_____
_____

2. Are the company's raw materials and/or other inputs readily available from multiple sources at competitive prices?
_____
_____

Where Do I Go From Here?

Action Items	Priority	Date	Who
1.			
2.			
3.			

12. Product/Service Quality

	Potential Value Impact (A)	Relevance (B)	Value Enhancement Score
	1 lowest to 10 highest	1 lowest to 10 highest	(A) + (B)
Score			
Business Operations Factors			

Reason for Importance: If a company can prove it has a quality product or service, buyers can view this as a competitive edge in the marketplace. In addition, a track record of quality products and/or services increases customer satisfaction and reduces customer returns, complaints, and similar issues that create costs or future liabilities for a buyer. For a company with a consistently high-quality product/service, buyers will typically consider market share growth, pricing growth, and a lower risk of customer turnover in their negotiations with a seller. Quality certifications, 6-Sigma designations, and other associations and testing serve to provide third-party evidence of a commitment to quality.

Where Do I Go From Here?

Self-Assessment of Your Company

1. Are the company's products or services high quality compared to competitive products/services?

_____

_____

2. Has the company received a quality certification?

_____

_____

3. What would be required to become a high-quality provider?

_____

_____

Action Items	Priority	Date	Who
1.			
2.			
3.			

13. Qualified and Competitively Paid Workforce

	Potential Value Impact (A)	**Relevance (B)**	**Value Enhancement Score**
	1 lowest to 10 highest	1 lowest to 10 highest	(A) + (B)
Score			
Business Operations Factors			

Reason for Importance: A company is the sum of its employees and accordingly buyers spend considerable time assessing their risks and opportunities in relation to a company's workforce, especially if the buyer is a strategic player. Accordingly, buyers will assess if the company has an ample source of qualified and competitively priced labor. They will also assess if employees are well trained and motivated, and if the salaries and hourly pay are in line with comparable jobs in the geographic area and/or the industry

In instances where the company has not paid employees an amount a buyer would reasonably expect to pay (i.e., no pay raises for years, overworked staff, etc.), the buyer may adjust the purchase price to reflect the normal wages they would anticipate paying post-closing.

Where Do I Go From Here?

Self-Assessment of Your Company

1. Does the company have an ample source of qualified and competitively priced labor?

_____

_____

2. Are employees well trained and motivated?

_____

_____

3. Are salaries and hourly pay in line with comparable jobs in the geographic area and the company's industry?

_____

_____

4. Is the company's employee turnover rate reasonable compared to the industry?

_____

_____

Action Items	Priority	Date	Who
1.			
2.			
3.			

14. Competitive Employee Benefits and Cost

	Potential Value Impact (A)	**Relevance (B)**	**Value Enhancement Score**
	1 lowest to 10 highest	1 lowest to 10 highest	(A) + (B)
Score			
Business Operations Factors			

Reason for Importance: A buyer will assess a seller's benefit costs compared to the geographic area or industry. If the benefit costs are lower than market there is a risk the costs will increase to retain and attract quality employees. If the costs are above market then there is the potential that the seller's cost structure is at a competitive disadvantage.

Self-Assessment of Your Company

1. How does the company's benefit program compare to that offered by other industry players?

_____

_____

2. What is the employees' consensus regarding the company's benefit program?

_____

_____

Where Do I Go From Here?

Action Items	Priority	Date	Who
1.			
2.			
3.			

15. Union

	Potential Value Impact (A)	Relevance (B)	Value Enhancement Score
	1 lowest to 10 highest	1 lowest to 10 highest	(A) + (B)
Score			
Business Operations Factors			

Reason for Importance: Buyers normally prefer a non-unionized workforce as unions have significantly more leverage and costs and require more formal procedures and complexities than a non-unionized workforce. If the company's labor force is unionized then a buyer will want to verify there is a history of good relations with the union with no strikes. In addition, the buyer will want to determine when the company's union contract is set to expire if the company is a party to a multi-employer pension plan.

Self-Assessment of Your Company

1. Is the company's labor force unionized?

_____

_____

2. If the company is organized, is there a history of good relations with the union and no strikes?

_____

_____

3. If organized, is the company's union contract set to expire within the next two years?

_____

_____

4. Is the company a party to a multi-employer pension plan?

_____

_____

Action Items	Priority	Date	Who
1.			
2.			
3.			

16. Facilities

	Potential Value Impact (A)	**Relevance (B)**	**Value Enhancement Score**
	1 lowest to 10 highest	1 lowest to 10 highest	(A) + (B)
Score			
Business Operations Factors			

Reason for Importance: A buyer's objective is to determine if capital expenditures are necessary and at what level to maintain or grow the business, which will influence their cash flow projections and offer price. Touring the company's facilities, buyers assess management style, discipline, reinvestment approach, and capacity utilization. They evaluate cleanliness, maintenance, growth potential, compliance with regulations, and the facility's layout. If the property is owned, buyers will inquire about the possibility of purchasing or leasing it and may request a recent appraisal. If leased, they will review the lease terms and renewal options. Buyers also consider the collateral value of equipment for financing, seeking recent appraisals if available.

Self-Assessment of Your Company

1. Are the company's land and buildings clean, well-maintained, and in compliance with all building codes and regulations?

_____

_____

Where Do I Go From Here?

2. Do the company's facilities demonstrate an efficient layout?

3. Is there room for expansion within the existing facilities?

4. If owned, are you open to either selling or leasing the facility to the buyer?

5. Is a recent appraisal available?

6. If the company's facilities are leased, is the remaining term of the lease five years or less (including renewal options)?

Action Items	Priority	Date	Who
1.			
2.			
3.			

17. Websites

	Potential Value Impact (A)	Relevance (B)	Value Enhancement Score
	1 lowest to 10 highest	1 lowest to 10 highest	(A) + (B)
Score			
Business Operations Factors			

Reason for Importance: Websites are often the first place the marketplace visits to become familiar with a company and first impressions are crucial to attract customers, employees, and vendors. In addition, websites offer companies an efficient communication and transactional vehicle. Thus, buyers will be looking for an attractive, easy-to-navigate, up-to-date, integrated website that is aligned with the company's fully developed marketing strategy.

Where Do I Go From Here?

Self-Assessment of Your Company

1. Is the company's website attractive, easy to navigate, and up-to-date?

_____

_____

2. Is the website part of a fully developed marketing strategy?

_____

_____

3. Does the company offer a communication and transaction website for customers, employees, and vendors?

_____

_____

Action Items	Priority	Date	Who
1.			
2.			
3.			

18. Track Record

	Potential Value Impact (A)	**Relevance (B)**	**Value Enhancement Score**
	1 lowest to 10 highest	1 lowest to 10 highest	(A) + (B)
Score			
Business Operations Factors			

Reason for Importance: A company's historical track record provides credibility to a seller's representation of the potential future benefits. If a company has a consistent record of growth in both sales and profits over the last several years and these are equal to or better than the overall industry, then buyers typically will justify a higher price.

Self-Assessment of Your Company

1. Does the company have a consistent record of growth in both sales and profits over the last several years?

_____

_____

2. Have sales growth and profit margins been equal to or better than the overall industry?

_____

_____

Where Do I Go From Here?

Action Items	Priority	Date	Who
1.			
2.			
3.			

19. Cyclicality

	Potential Value Impact (A)	Relevance (B)	Value Enhancement Score
	1 lowest to 10 highest	1 lowest to 10 highest	(A) + (B)
Score			
Financial Factors			

Reason for Importance: If the company's revenue is cyclical then the state of the economy and its outlook will be a key factor for buyers in determining their purchase price.

A seller will want to look for opportunities to offset this cyclicality with non-cyclical revenues to reduce risk and provide income during downtrends. For example, a building contractor could add preventative maintenance contracts to their revenue mix. If a seller's revenue is cyclical then a seller's exit value is typically maximized by timing their exit for periods during economic expansion.

Where Do I Go From Here?

Self-Assessment of Your Company

1. Are the company's revenues affected by domestic or global economic cycles?

_____

_____

2. If so, what is the economic outlook?

_____

_____

3. If "the stars are not aligned" – will you let the timing of your desired exit or the timing of the business cycle (and resulting value) drive your decision process?

_____

_____

Action Items	Priority	Date	Who
1.			
2.			
3.			

20. Seasonality

	Potential Value Impact (A)	**Relevance (B)**	**Value Enhancement Score**
	1 lowest to 10 highest	1 lowest to 10 highest	(A) + (B)
Score			
Financial Factors			

Reason for Importance: Working capital is a key component buyers analyze in valuing a company, especially so if a business is seasonal as working capital is typically needed during ramp up periods. Businesses can minimize this working capital drain by proactively and strategically planning for these periods. If a company can minimize the working capital required during these phases then a seller will typically be rewarded with an increased selling price.

Where Do I Go From Here?

Self-Assessment of Your Company

1. Do monthly sales, expenses, and working capital requirements vary significantly throughout the year?

_____

_____

2. If so, what are the drivers?

_____

_____

3. Do you project working capital requirements as part of your strategic and/or business plan?

_____

_____

Action Items	Priority	Date	Who
1.			
2.			
3.			

21. Revenue Size

Score	Potential Value Impact (A)	Relevance (B)	Value Enhancement Score
	1 lowest to 10 highest	1 lowest to 10 highest	(A) + (B)
Financial Factors			

Reason for Importance: In the middle market, larger companies usually can expect to receive a larger price multiple as the theory is that larger companies have lower risk and there is a greater buyer pool. This is often referred to as M&A financial arbitrage. Thus, a company with $100M in revenues will typically demand a higher price multiple than a company with $15M. Thus, companies should examine the M&A activity in their industry and determine the pricing thresholds and, if logical, incorporate into their strategies exit planning and timing. One common metric private equality firms consider is if the company's revenues are in the upper half of all competitors in the industry. If not, they want to evaluate if the company is of sufficient size that it could serve as a "platform" for consolidating several smaller companies in the industry.

Where Do I Go From Here?

Self-Assessment of Your Company

1. Are the company's revenues in the upper half of all competitors in the industry?

_____

_____

2. If not, is the company of sufficient size that it could serve as a "platform" for consolidating several companies in the industry?

_____

_____

Action Items	Priority	Date	Who
1.			
2.			
3.			

22. Business Plan

	Potential Value Impact (A)	Relevance (B)	Value Enhancement Score
	1 lowest to 10 highest	1 lowest to 10 highest	(A) + (B)
Score			
Financial Factors			

Reason for Importance: Buyers consider a documented business plan to be an important document. The business plan supports the growth projections. It documents the assumptions behind the projections and outlines the strategy and the costs of implementing the plan. A business plan also indicates that the selling company is managed well and provides a view into the strategic thinking of management. The document is also of importance to the buyer in preparation for bank loan documentation. The business plan's impact on value can be substantial. Without a plan, the selling company would be challenged by buyers on sales growth beyond industry averages. A well-constructed plan that supports higher growth projections can convince the buyer that the company is worth more and the financiers that is a viable transaction to fund. This is especially true if you have plans from prior years, along with the results you achieved. Being able to substantiate "This is what we said we were going to do and here is our result" will lend credibility to your current projections and assumptions.

Where Do I Go From Here?

Self-Assessment of Your Company

1. Does the company have a documented business plan for the next three to five years?

_____

_____

2. Is the plan comprehensive and defensible with specific and measurable objectives?

_____

_____

3. Does the plan include all the necessary action steps along with costs and investments to implement the plan?

_____

_____

Action Items	Priority	Date	Who
1.			
2.			
3.			

23. Operating Margins

	Potential Value Impact (A)	**Relevance (B)**	**Value Enhancement Score**
	1 lowest to 10 highest	1 lowest to 10 highest	(A) + (B)
Score			
Financial Factors			

Reason for Importance: Operating margins in line with industry standards indicate to a buyer that the business is running within some acceptable parameters. Low operating margins may indicate that some of the costs of expenses are too high, and although this may offer an opportunity to a buyer, it may also be a comment on the management team that the buyer is taking on. High margins on the other hand also need to be investigated carefully as, depending on the industry and business, they may indicate that the company is neglecting issues such as research and development or sales and marketing expenses, and this in turn could have negative impacts on future growth and operations. Great variability in operating margins is indicative of company risk. Margin trends are important as they may provide insights into the future profitability of the business.

Where Do I Go From Here?

Self-Assessment of Your Company

1. Are the company's operating margins equal to or better than industry norms?

   _____
   _____

2. Have margins been stable or improving over the last several years?

   _____
   _____

3. Have margin improvements been identified and evidenced with executable plans to achieve them?

   _____
   _____

Action Items	Priority	Date	Who
1.			
2.			
3.			

24. Capital Expenditures

	Potential Value Impact (A)	Relevance (B)	Value Enhancement Score
	1 lowest to 10 highest	1 lowest to 10 highest	(A) + (B)
Score			
Financial Factors			

Reason for Importance: Buyers buy the expected free cash flow that a business will provide. As such they need a clear idea of the capital expenditure required to sustain operations and support growth. The amounts projected should be tied into a business and/or strategic plan.

Where Do I Go From Here?

Self-Assessment of Your Company

1. Are the company's annual capital expenditure requirements relatively low?

_____

_____

2. Does the company anticipate any major capital expenditures to support current operations or future growth?

_____

_____

3. Does the company have a capital budgeting and approval process?

_____

_____

Action Items	Priority	Date	Who
1.			
2.			
3.			

25. Financial Statements

	Potential Value Impact (A)	Relevance (B)	Value Enhancement Score
	1 lowest to 10 highest	1 lowest to 10 highest	(A) + (B)
Score			
Financial Factors			

Reason for Importance: Audited financial statements indicate to a buyer that the financials presented are consistent with GAAP (Generally Accepted Accounting Principles) accounting standards. As a result, the buyer believes that the numbers truly reflect the financial condition of the company and there is negligible risk that a thorough review will produce "surprises." In the case of compiled or reviewed financial statements, the buyer's level of confidence is reduced. With audited statements, a buyer also avoids having to spend more time and money conducting his own audit during due diligence. From the seller's viewpoint, audited statements significantly reduce the chance for purchase price adjustments. Price adjustments often occur when costs such as accrued vacation expenses or allowances for doubtful accounts are taken against profits when the compiled or reviewed statements are changed to a GAAP basis. The impact of these adjustments can be substantial. For example, if GAAP accounting required that an allowance for doubtful accounts of 1% of revenues be added to the selling company's costs, the impact on a $10 million company would be a $100,000 reduction in profits. If the buyer were paying a purchase price of 5 times earnings, the purchase price reduction would be $500,000.

Where Do I Go From Here?

Self-Assessment of Your Company

1. Does the company have audited financial statements?

   _____
   _____

2. If not audited, are financial statements being prepared consistent with GAAP?

   _____
   _____

3. Are financial statements prepared timely and consistently?

   _____
   _____

Action Items	Priority	Date	Who
1.			
2.			
3.			

26. Customer Base/Quality of Revenue

	Potential Value Impact (A)	Relevance (B)	Value Enhancement Score
	1 lowest to 10 highest	1 lowest to 10 highest	(A) + (B)
Score			
Financial Factors			

Reason for Importance: Buyers prefer companies with recurring revenue and a diverse customer base. The customer profile is crucial, influencing factors like pricing flexibility, credit risk, growth opportunities, and production costs. During due diligence, buyers often analyze multi-year sales and margins to assess consistent, recurring revenue streams post-closing. Buyers typically pay for the expected future benefits, not just historical results. Companies with a broad, repeat customer base or long-term contracts offer more stability and predictability, reducing buyer risk and increasing valuation. In contrast, businesses reliant on one-time customers face higher risk and lower valuations. Stable referral relationships also support accurate revenue and earnings forecasts.

Where Do I Go From Here?

Self-Assessment of Your Company

1. Does the company have any strategic or long-term agreements with customers?
_____
_____

2. Do any of the company's customers account for more than 10% of revenue?
_____
_____

3. Does the company have a long history with its major customers?
_____
_____

4. Are new customers being added continuously?
_____
_____

5. Are the company's customers consumers, retailers, or corporations?
_____
_____

Action Items	Priority	Date	Who
1.			
2.			
3.			

27. Company Records

	Potential Value Impact (A)	Relevance (B)	Value Enhancement Score
	1 lowest to 10 highest	1 lowest to 10 highest	(A) + (B)
Score			
Financial Factors			

Reason for Importance: Buyers demand accurate and sufficient financial and non-financial information when they are considering a purchase or when performing their pre-sale due diligence. If a company's records are insufficient or aren't in order this can create a sellability issue, reduce the price a buyer is willing to pay, or a buyer will want advantageous terms. Many companies that plan for a transition begin a process of internal due diligence and start storing company records in an "online vault" or specific area on their server.

Where Do I Go From Here?

Self-Assessment of Your Company

1. Are the company's records in good order and easily accessible?

_____
_____

2. How much time and effort would it require to assemble all the company's current contracts?

_____
_____

3. How much time and effort would it require to access specific transactional records (i.e., customer or vendor invoices, bank statements, etc.) from two years ago?

_____
_____

Action Items	Priority	Date	Who
1.			
2.			
3.			

28. Financial Controls

	Potential Value Impact (A)	Relevance (B)	Value Enhancement Score
	1 lowest to 10 highest	1 lowest to 10 highest	(A) + (B)
Score			
Financial Factors			

Reason for Importance: A company's internal financial controls play a key role in preventing and detecting fraud and protecting the organization's resources, both physical (e.g., machinery and property) and intangible (e.g., reputation or intellectual property such as trademarks). At the organizational level, internal control objectives relate to the reliability of financial reporting, timely feedback on the achievement of operational or strategic goals, and compliance with laws and regulations. At the specific transaction level, internal control refers to the actions taken to achieve a specific objective (e.g., how to ensure the organization's payments to third parties are for valid services rendered.) Internal control procedures reduce process variation, leading to more predictable outcomes. If a seller has good financial internal controls in place this typically results in greater financial performance and also reduces a buyer's risk. Both correlate to a higher price for a seller

Self-Assessment of Your Company

1. Does the company have documented internal controls?

_____

_____

2. Who monitors and verifies that sufficient controls are in place and working?

_____

_____

3. Has the company ever incurred a monetary loss due to a lack of internal controls?

_____

_____

Action Items	Priority	Date	Who
1.			
2.			
3.			

29. Opportunity for Growth

	Potential Value Impact (A)	**Relevance (B)**	**Value Enhancement Score**
	1 lowest to 10 highest	1 lowest to 10 highest	(A) + (B)
Score			
Financial Factors			

Reason for Importance: Buyers seek out companies with significant and feasible opportunities for growth. Growth opportunities that have been identified and evidenced with executable plans to achieve them are usually reflected in the price a buyer is willing to pay for a business. These opportunities are best disclosed and tracked via a strategic and/or business plan.

Self-Assessment of Your Company

1. Have significant and feasible opportunities for growth been identified?

_____

_____

2. Are plans in place and have preliminary actions been taken to implement them?

_____

_____

3. Are profit margins associated with growth opportunities consistent or better than the company's historical margins?

_____

_____

Action Items	Priority	Date	Who
1.			
2.			
3.			

30. Corporate Structure

	Potential Value Impact (A)	**Relevance (B)**	**Value Enhancement Score**
	1 lowest to 10 highest	1 lowest to 10 highest	(A) + (B)
Score			
Financial Factors			

Reason for Importance: "S" corporations or LLCs (pass-through entities) allow buyers to purchase assets of a company instead of the stock without subjecting the seller to "double" taxation, and thus they are inherently a favorable entity for a buyer versus "C" corporations because the parties' tax motivations aren't contradictory. When purchasing assets, a buyer can "write-up" the assets and reduce income taxes either through increased depreciation or higher cost of sales. Under a stock sale, the buyer receives no benefits since the purchase price simply establishes the buyer's stock basis and only provides capital gains tax savings when the stock is sold in the future. In addition, buyers prefer to purchase the assets of a company to avoid any unknown liabilities that would be their responsibility with the purchase of the company's stock.

Where Do I Go From Here?

Self-Assessment of Your Company

1. Do you have multiple companies that you use for asset protection?

_____

_____

2. What type of entity is your "main" company?

_____

_____

3. If a C corporation, have you explored converting into another entity type?

_____

_____

Action Items	Priority	Date	Who
1.			
2.			
3.			

31. Board of Directors/Advisors

	Potential Value Impact (A)	Relevance (B)	Value Enhancement Score
	1 lowest to 10 highest	1 lowest to 10 highest	(A) + (B)
Score			
Legal/Regulatory Factors			

Reason for Importance: An active and respected board of directors/advisors is an asset to a company in several ways. The board can be a sounding board for company initiatives and can offer advice and guidance. It can also be a source for business contacts and innovative ideas. To the extent that a Board can improve a company's performance, the value of the business will increase. In addition, an active board adds credibility to the company's business plans and its overall management.

Where Do I Go From Here?

Self-Assessment of Your Company

1. Does the company have a board of credible outside directors or advisors in place that consult with you regarding major decisions of the company?

_____

_____

2. Do your advisors have certain expertise or contacts that provide strategic value to the company?

_____

_____

3. Are you meeting regularly?

_____

_____

Action Items	Priority	Date	Who
1.			
2.			
3.			

32. Environmental Issues

	Potential Value Impact (A)	**Relevance (B)**	**Value Enhancement Score**
	1 lowest to 10 highest	1 lowest to 10 highest	(A) + (B)
Score			
Legal/Regulatory Factors			

Reason for Importance: Environmental issues are one of the primary reasons for transactions not closing. The reason is uncertainty. Unless a problem, such as ground contamination or excess air emissions, is cleaned up and the remediation is officially approved by the proper environmental agency, the extent of future fines and cleanup costs are not fully known. Often the risk is too great for the buyer to complete the transaction. Even if the buyer is satisfied, banks providing financing for the transaction are normally extremely cautious about environmental problems and will not provide a loan until the issue is resolved. Sellers also have a vested interest in removing uncertainty relating to environmental issues, as they are in many cases required to make representations and warranties on environmental risks.

Where Do I Go From Here?

Self-Assessment of Your Company

1. Are there any known or suspected environmental issues associated with the company's facilities or property?

_____

_____

2. Are you familiar with the entire history of the property?

_____

_____

3. If potential environmental issues may exist, have you conducted the necessary studies and any remediation and received final regulatory approvals?

_____

_____

Action Items	Priority	Date	Who
1.			
2.			
3.			

33. Leases and Other Contracts

	Potential Value Impact (A)	**Relevance (B)**	**Value Enhancement Score**
	1 lowest to 10 highest	1 lowest to 10 highest	(A) + (B)
Score			
Legal/Regulatory Factors			

Reason for Importance: A buyer's cash flow and ability to operate in the same or greater capacity as the seller is essential in securing a deal. Accordingly, buyers will need to confirm the company's leases and other contracts are assignable, won't place undue restrictions on the buyer, and contract costs aren't above current market prices.

Where Do I Go From Here?

Self-Assessment of Your Company

1. Are the company's leases and other contracts assignable or would they place restrictions on a new owner?

_____

_____

2. Is the rent the company pays on its building comparable to local market rates?

_____

_____

3. How will non assignable contracts affect a new owner?

_____

_____

Action Items	Priority	Date	Who
1.			
2.			
3.			

34. Lawsuits

	Potential Value Impact (A)	Relevance (B)	Value Enhancement Score
	1 lowest to 10 highest	1 lowest to 10 highest	(A) + (B)
Score			
Legal/Regulatory Factors			

Reason for Importance: The presence of current or historical lawsuits for a company automatically raises a red flag for buyers and they perceive such as a potential risk. This could threaten a seller's negotiation leverage regarding price, terms, and deal structure. If the nature, quantity, legal costs, and/or outcome of the lawsuits are outside ordinary industry norms then this could create sellability issues for a seller.

Where Do I Go From Here?

Self-Assessment of Your Company

1. Does the company have any current lawsuits or a history of lawsuits?

_____

_____

2. Is there a threat of future lawsuits?

_____

_____

3. Has the company addressed the root cause of the lawsuits?

_____

_____

Action Items	Priority	Date	Who
1.			
2.			
3.			

35. Taxes

	Potential Value Impact (A)	Relevance (B)	Value Enhancement Score
	1 lowest to 10 highest	1 lowest to 10 highest	(A) + (B)
Score			
Legal/Regulatory Factors			

Reason for Importance: If a company is not current on all tax filings or payments it automatically raises a red flag for buyers. Buyers typically assume the company has solvency and/or internal control issues. Both create doubt by buyers and could impair the sellability or negotiation leverage of a seller. In addition, a Certificate of Good Tax Standing is a normal pre-condition of closing, so if there are issues this could delay or stop the transaction. Secondly, if the company has been audited by the IRS or the state, this has the potential to create the same scenario unless the company received a clean report.

Where Do I Go From Here?

Self-Assessment of Your Company

1. Is the company current on all tax filings and tax payments?

   _____

   _____

2. Has the company been audited by the IRS or state and what was the finding of the report?

   _____

   _____

3. Have you requested a tax clearance certificate from the states in which the company does business?

   _____

   _____

Action Items	Priority	Date	Who
1.			
2.			
3.			

36. OSHA

	Potential Value Impact (A)	Relevance (B)	Value Enhancement Score
	1 lowest to 10 highest	1 lowest to 10 highest	(A) + (B)
Score			
Legal/Regulatory Factors			

Reason for Importance: If a company has had an OSHA inspection in the last few years and the findings identified needed improvements, buyers will want to confirm the needed improvements have been completed so they don't inherit the risk. If the company has a history of OSHA inspections and fines, then rational buyers will assume a heightened level of risk and/or additional costs to prevent future fines. Thus, it would negatively affect a buyer's perception of value and price.

Self-Assessment of Your Company

1. Has the company had an OSHA inspection in the last three years?

_____

_____

2. What were the findings?

_____

_____

3. If the review identified needed improvements, have all been completed?

_____

_____

4. Does the company have a history of OSHA fines?

_____

_____

Action Items	Priority	Date	Who
1.			
2.			
3.			

37. OSHA

	Potential Value Impact (A)	Relevance (B)	Value Enhancement Score
	1 lowest to 10 highest	1 lowest to 10 highest	(A) + (B)
Score			
Legal/Regulatory Factors			

Reason for Importance: Buyers typically aren't willing to assume any risk for events that occurred before their date of ownership. Liability claims are often made months if not years after the event that created the liability occurred. Accordingly, sellers will be at risk for any event that happens before closing. If a seller has adequate insurance coverage to cover potential liability and the liability insurance coverage is on an "occurrence" rather than a "claims made" basis then buyers typically won't require risk protection via a reduced price, advantageous deal terms, or structure.

Self-Assessment of Your Company

1. Does the company have sufficient insurance in place to cover potential liability?

_____

_____

2. Is insurance coverage on an "occurrence" rather than a "claims made" basis?

_____

_____

Action Items	Priority	Date	Who
1.			
2.			
3.			

38. Intellectual Property

	Potential Value Impact (A)	Relevance (B)	Value Enhancement Score
	1 lowest to 10 highest	1 lowest to 10 highest	(A) + (B)
Score			
Legal/Regulatory Factors			

Reason for Importance: Companies that protect their revenue and profit streams via patents, trademarks, and properly registered copyrights typically reduce competitive risks for buyers. In the case of patents, patents with over half of their original life remaining are preferable to buyers. If any of the patents, trademarks, or registered copyrights are infringed upon and aren't enforced by a company then such intellectual property's value can be perceived as negligible by a buyer.

Where Do I Go From Here?

Self-Assessment of Your Company

1. Does the company have intangible assets such as patents, trademarks, and copyrights that have been properly registered and fully protected?

_____

_____

2. In the case of patents, does the patent have over half of its original life remaining?

_____

_____

3. Has anyone infringed on your intellectual property?

_____

_____

4. If so, were you able to cease such infringement?

_____

_____

Action Items	Priority	Date	Who
1.			
2.			
3.			

39. Non-Compete with Key Employees

	Potential Value Impact (A)	Relevance (B)	Value Enhancement Score
	1 lowest to 10 highest	1 lowest to 10 highest	(A) + (B)
Score			

Legal/Regulatory Factors

Reason for Importance: Buyers want protection so that key employees won't steal customers, employees, and other company intelligence post-sale to compete with the company. If a stock deal and non-compete agreements aren't in place, then buyers will typically attempt to protect their interests by reducing the purchase price or using advantageous deal terms and structure, shifting the risk to the seller. If an asset deal, then buyers will typically re-hire the seller's employees but will want assurances or executed non-compete agreements in place before closing for certain employees.

Self-Assessment of Your Company

1. Does the company have non-compete agreements with the management team and other sensitive areas such as the sales team?

_____

_____

2. Have the agreements been reviewed recently by your attorney?

_____

_____

3. If non-compete agreements aren't in place, which employees would a potential buyer want to compel into such an agreement and what, if any, incentive would be required?

_____

_____

Action Items	Priority	Date	Who
1.			
2.			
3.			

40. Barriers to Entry

	Potential Value Impact (A)	Relevance (B)	Value Enhancement Score
	1 lowest to 10 highest	1 lowest to 10 highest	(A) + (B)
Score			
Legal/Regulatory Factors			

Reason for Importance: Buyers value a business with significant barriers to entry because such barriers limit competition. Less competition reduces the business risk associated with the selling company and therefore has a positive effect on purchase price. Barriers to entry consist of capital costs necessary to enter the market, licenses, technology, patents, trademarks, etc.

Self-Assessment of Your Company

1. Describe the barriers to entry into your markets (capital, licenses, technology, etc.). What patents, registered trademarks or other protected intellectual property does the company own?

_____

_____

2. Are you aware of any infringements?

_____

_____

3. If so, have you pursued all legal remedies?

_____

_____

Action Items	Priority	Date	Who
1.			
2.			
3.			

41. Industry Consolidation

	Potential Value Impact (A)	Relevance (B)	Value Enhancement Score
	1 lowest to 10 highest	1 lowest to 10 highest	(A) + (B)
Score			

Reason for Importance: Is the company's industry undergoing consolidation in which smaller competitors are purchased and consolidated into larger companies to achieve benefits of scale and the elimination of duplicative costs? Depending on the stage, this factor could be positive or negative. If it's early enough in the business lifecycle, business ow ners may want to think about how to attract strategic buyers, as opposed to a financial buyer, as a way to maximize the selling price. Strategic buyers typically can justify a higher price, especially if the company can be used as part of the platform for consolidation.

If at a late stage, then a seller's negotiation leverage is typically reduced unless a good strategic fit. If at a post-consolidation stage then generally a seller can be at a disadvantage as the consolidated companies will have greater resources, purchasing power, efficiencies, etc.

Where Do I Go From Here?

Self-Assessment of Your Company

1. Is the company's industry undergoing consolidation in which smaller competitors are purchased and consolidated into larger companies to achieve benefits of scale and the elimination of duplicative costs?

_____

_____

2. If "the stars are not aligned" – will you let the timing of your desired exit or the value you will receive drive your decision process?

_____

_____

Action Items	Priority	Date	Who
1.			
2.			
3.			

42. Industry Outlook

	Potential Value Impact (A)	Relevance (B)	Value Enhancement Score
	1 lowest to 10 highest	1 lowest to 10 highest	(A) + (B)
Score			
Industry/Market Factors			

Reason for Importance: A company's industry outlook creates the underlying tone for buyers' interest and the corresponding M&A activity in the industry. Buyers prefer industries where the outlook is favorable in terms of growth, profit margins, competition, legislation, etc. Similarly, if your industry is regulated, buyers want a sense of certainty around pending legislated changes.

Self-Assessment of Your Company

1. Is the company's future favorable in terms of the industry's future growth projections, profit margins, competition, legislation, etc.?

_____

_____

2. Is there pending legislation or discussion around policies that would positively or negatively impact your company?

_____

_____

Where Do I Go From Here?

Action Items	Priority	Date	Who
1.			
2.			
3.			

43. Industry Information

	Potential Value Impact (A)	Relevance (B)	Value Enhancement Score
	1 lowest to 10 highest	1 lowest to 10 highest	(A) + (B)
Score			
Industry/Market Factors			

Reason for Importance: A buyer's perceived risk is reduced if there is readily available information on the industry from industry associations or business press including growth projections, industry trends, competitors, etc.

Self-Assessment of Your Company

1. Is information on the company's industry readily available from industry associations or business press including growth projections, industry trends, competitors, etc.

_____
_____

2. Do you compile this information and integrate it into your strategic and/or business plans?

_____
_____

Where Do I Go From Here?

Action Items	Priority	Date	Who
1.			
2.			
3.			

44. Market Position

Score	Potential Value Impact (A)	Relevance (B)	Value Enhancement Score
	1 lowest to 10 highest	1 lowest to 10 highest	(A) + (B)
Score			
Industry/Market Factors			

Reason for Importance: If a company has a strong market position, a protected niche product or service, a well-known brand(s), and/or excellent reputation this ordinarily equates to higher barriers of entry and a competitive advantage and accordingly justifies a higher price by buyers.

Self-Assessment of Your Company

1. Does your company have a strong market share or protected niche in the industry?

_____

_____

2. Does the company have a well-known brand name and excellent reputation?

_____

_____

3. How do you measure or benchmark your company to the industry?

_____

_____

Action Items	Priority	Date	Who
1.			
2.			
3.			

45. Product/Service Obsolesce

	Potential Value Impact (A)	Relevance (B)	Value Enhancement Score
	1 lowest to 10 highest	1 lowest to 10 highest	(A) + (B)
Score			
Industry/Market Factors			

Reason for Importance: Buyers aren't buying the historical benefit streams of the seller, they are purchasing the future benefit stream. Thus, buyers desire a favorable long-term outlook for the seller's products or services that is not threatened by technological obsolescence or global competition.

Self-Assessment of Your Company

1. Does the company have a favorable long-term outlook for its products or services that is not threatened by technological obsolescence or global competition?

_____

_____

2. If you believe there is no threat, describe why this is the case.

_____

_____

Where Do I Go From Here?

Action Items	Priority	Date	Who
1.			
2.			
3.			

46. Industry Metrics

	Potential Value Impact (A)	**Relevance (B)**	**Value Enhancement Score**
	1 lowest to 10 highest	1 lowest to 10 highest	(A) + (B)
Score			
	Industry/Market Factors		

Reason for Importance: A company that meets or exceeds its industry's average financial metrics is perceived as a stronger and less risky company and typically can demand a higher price. A comparison of a company's financial metrics to their industry is a valuable periodic exercise as it identifies how a company compares to its peers and identifies opportunities for improvement. Common financial metrics used in comparison would include accounts receivable days sales outstanding, accounts payable days payable, inventory days' supply, gross and operating margins, growth rates, etc.

Where Do I Go From Here?

Self-Assessment of Your Company

1. How do your company's financial metrics compare to your industry?

2. Have you identified opportunities for improvement using this exercise?

3. Do you use these metrics as a benchmark for your management team?

Action Items	Priority	Date	Who
1.			
2.			
3.			

47. M&A Markets

	Potential Value Impact (A)	Relevance (B)	Value Enhancement Score
	1 lowest to 10 highest	1 lowest to 10 highest	(A) + (B)
Score			
Industry/Market Factors			

Reason for Importance: If the merger and acquisition (M&A) marketplace is highly active in the company's industry this is generally the best time for a seller to exit if they are prepared and positioned to do so. There are a variety of factors that impact M&A activity, such as tax laws, interest rates, and the economic outlook.

Where Do I Go From Here?

Self-Assessment of Your Company

1. Is the merger and acquisition (M&A) market in the company's industry positive including ready availability of financing, low interest rates, and favorable tax laws?

_____

_____

2. Are both financial and strategic buyers actively acquiring companies?

_____

_____

3. What are the value factors that the active strategic acquirers are seeking (i.e., geographic footprint, technology, customer network, etc.)?

_____

_____

Action Items	Priority	Date	Who
1.			
2.			
3.			

48. Economy

	Potential Value Impact (A)	**Relevance (B)**	**Value Enhancement Score**
	1 lowest to 10 highest	1 lowest to 10 highest	(A) + (B)
Score			
Economic/M&A Factors			

Reason for Importance: The direction of the economy, in the markets that a company operates, typically governs the outlook for a company's products or services. Accordingly, buyers prefer economic cycles pointed in the direction that benefits a company's products and services.

Self-Assessment of Your Company

1. In the markets that the company operates, is the economy expanding or contracting?

_____

_____

2. What are the indicators (i.e., interest rates and the stock indexes) stating and what is the consensus outlook?

_____

_____

Where Do I Go From Here?

Action Items	Priority	Date	Who
1.			
2.			
3.			

49. Age/Motivation of Owner(s)

	Potential Value Impact (A)	Relevance (B)	Value Enhancement Score
	1 lowest to 10 highest	1 lowest to 10 highest	(A) + (B)
Score			
Economic/M&A Factors			

Reason for Importance: One of the first questions buyers often ask is why the business owner is selling. They want to know what the owner's motivation is to sell so that they can be assured that the seller is serious about selling. Investigating and negotiating a potential acquisition is expensive including travel, legal, accounting, and other expenses as well as the buyer's time. The buyer wants to be sure that the seller is acting in good faith and is not just "testing the market." If the owner is over 55 years old, a specific exit plan goes a long way in establishing that the owner is serious. If the owner is under 55, he should have either an exit plan that outlines what he will do after he leaves the business or be committed to staying with the business for several years. With specific plans in place for the owner, the buyer can be more confident that the owner will not change his mind before closing. Since any buyer has a limited amount of time and money, a buyer will gravitate toward businesses where the seller's motivation to sell is earnest and unambiguous.

Where Do I Go From Here?

Self-Assessment of Your Company

1. What is motivating you to consider an exit?
_____
_____

2. How would you describe this to a potential suitor?
_____
_____

3. What evidence can you provide to show you are motivated (exit plan, valuation, etc.)?
_____
_____

Action Items	Priority	Date	Who
1.			
2.			
3.			

50. Attitude of Owner(s)

	Potential Value Impact (A)	Relevance (B)	Value Enhancement Score
	1 lowest to 10 highest	1 lowest to 10 highest	(A) + (B)
Score			
Personal Factors			

Reason for Importance: Because buyers spend both time and money in the investigation and purchase of a company, they want to deal with a seller that is serious about the transaction, is trustworthy, and is easy to deal with. "Chemistry" or the intangible connection between the buyer and seller in many cases is often the deciding factor in whether or not a transaction is completed. While chemistry is a two-way street, a positive, friendly, and cooperative attitude by the seller will help in convincing the buyer that he is dealing with a person he can respect and trust. It's human nature to be attracted to someone with a positive and friendly attitude as opposed to someone with an evasive or negative attitude.

Where Do I Go From Here?

Self-Assessment of Your Company

1. Do you demonstrate a positive and cooperative attitude?
   _____
   _____

2. Are you enthusiastic and committed to the business's future?
   _____
   _____

3. Do you answer questions honestly and openly?
   _____
   _____

Action Items	Priority	Date	Who
1.			
2.			
3.			

51. Family/Partner Consensus

	Potential Value Impact (A)	Relevance (B)	Value Enhancement Score
	1 lowest to 10 highest	1 lowest to 10 highest	(A) + (B)
Score			
Personal Factors			

Reason for Importance: In addition to the practical reasons for having all shareholders in agreement regarding a sale of the business, shareholder consensus is also important to a buyer. Before spending both time and money on a potential transaction, buyers want assurance that all the shareholders will sell. If some shareholders want to sell and some do not, a buyer often will view pursuing the transaction as a waste of time. If the buyer still goes ahead with such a transaction, they will have to deal with the issue of minority shareholders and their eventual exit from the business, which complicates the transaction greatly. If all shareholders agree to sell, all these issues go away.

Where Do I Go From Here?

Self-Assessment of Your Company

1. Have **you** discussed your exit plans with your family and other shareholders?

   _____

   _____

2. Are they in agreement about your exit plan?

   _____

   _____

3. Do any family members or other shareholders have any hidden agendas?

   _____

   _____

Action Items	Priority	Date	Who
1.			
2.			
3.			

52. Reasonable Expectations of Value

	Potential Value Impact (A)	**Relevance (B)**	**Value Enhancement Score**
	1 lowest to 10 highest	1 lowest to 10 highest	(A) + (B)
Score			
Personal Factors			

Reason for Importance: Ultimately the price a buyer will pay has to make sense financially. Buyers' objectives such as return on investment, cash flow, or synergistic cost savings will determine the price they are willing to pay for a business. In some cases, however, business owners have unrealistic expectations for their business value. These expectations might result from applying high PIE multiples of a large public corporation in the same industry to their own company or hearing about a high-priced deal completed by a friend. Whatever the reason, buyers do not want to waste their time and money on pursuing a company in which the owner expects a price that is not achievable. When a seller has had a recent business evaluation or his expectations are in line with recent sale transactions in his industry, this concern is eliminated.

Where Do I Go From Here?

Self-Assessment of Your Company

1. Are your expectations in line with recent sales of comparable businesses?

_____

_____

2. Have you received a recent business appraisal from an independent third party?

_____

_____

3. Do you consider the appraised value acceptable?

_____

_____

Action Items	Priority	Date	Who
1.			
2.			
3.			

53. Open to Deal Structure

	Potential Value Impact (A)	**Relevance (B)**	**Value Enhancement Score**
	1 lowest to 10 highest	1 lowest to 10 highest	(A) + (B)
Score			
Personal Factors			

Reason for Importance: Deal structure is one of the most crucial factors in determining the sale price in a transaction. Because an all-cash transaction places the business risk entirely on the buyer's side, a buyer will be reluctant to offer as much for the business as when a seller is willing to share some of the risk. Another consideration is that a 100% cash transaction makes it more difficult to finance or to achieve the buyer's desired returns. Delayed or contingent payments, non-compete or consulting agreements, or asset versus stock deals are all deal structuring possibilities that help bridge the gap between the seller's price expectations and the buyer's willingness to pay. If the seller is willing to consider deal structure, then the buyer is more comfortable that he/she will be able to reach agreement on a deal. In all cases, however, whether structured or not, a seller must be willing to provide certain indemnifications and warranties to the buyer. Without any indemnifications and warranties, few buyers would be willing to purchase such a business.

Self-Assessment of Your Company

1. Do you understand the impact various deal structures may have on the amount of money you receive after taxes?

_____

_____

2. Are you insisting on an all-cash transaction or will you consider various forms of deal structure including seller notes, non-compete payments, consulting agreements, and/or earn-outs?

_____

_____

3. Are you willing to provide a buyer with the normal indemnifications and warranties that are typical in similar transactions?

_____

_____

Action Items	Priority	Date	Who
1.			
2.			
3.			

10 KEY STEPS FOR YOUR PERFECT EXIT

10 KEY STEPS FOR YOUR PERFECT EXIT

1. **Assemble your Team.**
   Have all your specialists lined up in advance.

2. **Don't negotiate the sale yourself.**
   "Only a fool would hire himself as his attorney."

3. **Don't negotiate the contracts with your advisors yourself.**
   Have someone who sits on your side of the table help you with all of these.

4. **Make sure your Fire Drill is in place.**
   The sale will occupy significant portions of your time.

5. **Organize all your financial records in one place.**
   A super organized business is eminently suleable. A disorganized one is not.

6. **Maintain confidentiality.**
   This is key to preventing disruption among employees, suppliers, customers, and competitors.

7. **Meet with your Key Advisors before you even go to market.**
   Knowledge is power.

8. **Design and Practice your presentation of your business.**
   The 5 P's. Why it will be even better in 3 years.

9. **Think like the buyer.**
   Follow the Golden Rule throughout.

10. **Rest up!**
    A sale is an arduous process.

PETER F. CULVER, J.D.
CHIEF WEALTH STRATEGIST | peter@freedomfamilyoffice.com

FREEDOM FAMILY OFFICE

With over 30 years of experience helping entrepreneurs navigate the pre-sale, post-sale journey.

(855) 540-0400   www.FreedomFamilyOffice.com   www.linkedin.com/company/freedom-family-office

TOP 10 MISTAKES AFTER YOUR 8-FIGURE EXITS

TOP 10 MISTAKES AFTER YOUR 8-FIGURE EXIT

1. **Failing to Take a Breather**
   There are many important decisions to make. Don't rush into any of them.

2. **Not Building Predictable Passive Income**
   Have a concrete plan for generating all the income that you need.

3. **Investing your money too soon - either in the market or in another business.**
   Plan first, then invest.

4. **Paying Too Much in Taxes**
   Don't let your wealth be confiscated by income and estate taxes.

5. **Letting Inflation Steal your Purchasing Power**
   This is another great confiscator of wealth. Address it now.

6. **Exposing Your Assets To Creditors**
   You now have a nest egg. Protect it from avoidable liabilities.

7. **Shortening Your Life Expectancy**
   Personal health is one of the biggest risks and expenses in later years. Get everything in place now.

8. **Not Building Your Ideal Life**
   There are many important decisions to make. Don't rush into any of them.

9. **Not Giving Back**
   Now you have the time and money to make an impact in new ways. Take advantage.

10. **Handing Over Your Assets to Unprepared Heirs**
    Work with them to become responsible stewards of your wealth.

PETER F. CULVER, J.D.
CHIEF WEALTH STRATEGIST | peter@freedomfamilyoffice.com

FREEDOM FAMILY OFFICE

With over 30 years of experience helping entrepreneurs navigate the pre-sale, post-sale journey.

(855) 540-0400 www.FreedomFamilyOffice.com www.linkedin.com/company/freedom-family-office

10 CRITICAL QUESTIONS TO ANSWER BEFORE YOU EXIT

10 CRITICAL QUESTIONS TO ANSWER BEFORE YOU EXIT

1. What is your business WORTH?
This is the key driver of a successful exit. Be sure you know.

2. Is this the RIGHT TIME to exit?
Is your business ready? Is the market ready? Are you ready?

3. Do you want to sell 100%, Control, or a Minority Interest?
How much you want to sell has a huge impact on how you structure the deal.

4. Who is the right buyer... Strategic Buyer, Financial Buyer, Management Buyout?
The type of Buyer you work with significantly impacts the terms of the deal.

5. How will you spend your time afterwards?
Always begin with the end in mind. What do you want to be doing after the sale?

6. How much money do you need at closing?
Don't sell your company before you have the detailed Money Map for life after the sale.

7. Do you want to pay capital gains taxes?
Have you considered all the ways to reduce taxes on the sales? Start early on this one.

8. What will you do with the cash?
There's a tendency to rush to deploy the sales proceeds. Take a breather!

9. What if you can't get what you want/need?
There are many important decisions to make. Don't rush into any of them.

10. Do you have a support network?
Selling is emotional - who will be your cool head throughout the process?

PETER F. CULVER, J.D.
peter@freedomfamilyoffice.com

FREEDOM FAMILY OFFICE

With over 30 years of experience helping entrepreneurs navigate the pre-sale, post-sale journey.

(855) 540-0400 | www.FreedomFamilyOffice.com | www.linkedin.com/company/freedom-family-office

FUTURE CONSIDERATIONS

"Knowledge is of no value unless you put it into practice."

— ANTON CHEKHOV

Technological Developments

Since 2013, technological advancements such as artificial intelligence (AI) and automation have revolutionized business operations, enabling companies to significantly increase efficiency, reduce operational costs, and develop innovative products and services. AI-driven analytics provide deep insights into customer behaviors and market trends, facilitating data-driven decision-making. Automation has streamlined processes in sectors like manufacturing and logistics, reducing human error and boosting productivity. Additionally, the gig economy has transformed workforce management, offering businesses access to a flexible and diverse talent pool. Embracing these technologies is essential for staying competitive in the modern business landscape. Companies that effectively integrate these advancements can not only enhance their operational efficiency but also position themselves as innovative leaders in their industries.

Remote Work Trends

The COVID-19 pandemic accelerated the shift to remote work, fundamentally changing business practices. Companies quickly adopted flexible work arrangements to maintain operations during lockdowns and social distancing measures. As of 2023, remote work remains a significant trend, with approximately 30% of the workforce working remotely at least part-time. This shift has demonstrated that remote work can enhance productivity, reduce overhead costs, and improve employee satisfaction. However, it also presents challenges such as maintaining company culture, ensuring effective communication, and implementing robust cybersecurity measures. Successfully navigating these challenges can enhance a business's adaptability and resilience. Companies that adopt flexible work policies and invest in the right technologies can attract top talent and foster a more engaged and satisfied workforce.

Entrepreneurship Trends

Recent years have seen a rise in social entrepreneurship and the gig economy, with more individuals launching businesses that prioritize social impact and flexible work arrangements. Social entrepreneurs focus on addressing societal challenges while achieving financial sustainability, leading to innovative solutions in areas such as healthcare, education, and environmental sustainability. The gig economy offers workers the flexibility to manage their schedules and work on diverse projects, appealing to a wide range of talent. These trends reflect a shift towards more purpose-driven and adaptable business models, which can attract passionate employees and loyal customers. Entrepreneurs embracing these trends can drive meaningful change while building financially successful enterprises.

Global Economic Conditions

Global economic conditions have been shaped by various significant factors, including trade wars, supply chain disruptions, and rising inflation. Trade wars have led to increased tariffs and regulatory challenges, affecting international business operations and profitability. Supply chain disruptions, exacerbated by the COVID-19 pandemic, have caused delays and increased costs for many businesses. Additionally, rising inflation rates have increased operational costs, squeezing profit margins and impacting pricing strategies. Business owners must navigate these complex economic conditions with strategic planning and adaptability to maintain stability and growth. Understanding these global dynamics is crucial for making informed decisions and securing the long-term success of your business.

Diversity and Inclusion in Business

There has been a growing emphasis on diversity and inclusion within the business world. Companies are increasingly recognizing that diverse leadership teams and inclusive work environments are crucial for driving innovation and achieving business success. Diverse teams bring a variety of perspectives and ideas, leading to more creative solutions and better decision-making. Furthermore, inclusive workplaces enhance employee satisfaction and retention, fostering a positive corporate culture. Businesses committed to diversity and inclusion can attract top talent and build stronger, more resilient organizations. Embracing diversity and inclusion not only aligns with ethical business practices but also contributes to a more dynamic and innovative business environment.

Environmental, Social, and Governance (ESG) Factors

Environmental, social, and governance (ESG) factors have become critical considerations for businesses and investors alike. As of 2023, companies are increasingly adopting ESG practices to enhance sustainability, social responsibility, and corporate governance. Implementing ESG strategies can lead to better risk management, improved financial performance, and increased investor confidence. For example, businesses that prioritize environmental sustainability can reduce costs through energy efficiency and waste reduction. Socially responsible practices, such as fair labor policies and community engagement, enhance brand reputation. Strong corporate governance ensures ethical behavior and accountability, which is vital for long-term success. Integrating ESG considerations into a business strategy can help build a sustainable and socially responsible enterprise that is well-regarded by stakeholders.

RESOURCES FOR READERS

If you want to learn more on your own, here are two recommendations:

1. Follow us on social media platforms where we share insights, market updates, and other information helpful to entrepreneurs. Search Freedom Family Office on:

   - Facebook/Meta
   - LinkedIn
   - YouTube
   - Instagram

2. Visit www.FreedomFamilyOffice.com and go to our Free Resources section. You can find whitepapers and articles of interest to people like you.

If you'd like to find ways to implement the ideas in this book, please email Hello@freedomfamilyoffice.com to join us for:

- Our online workshop "Creating Your Ideal Work Week"—a 90-minute course where you will discover an innovative approach to productivity

- Your personal financial assessment—to get clarity on how much money you need from your business to achieve financial security

- Your "Sellability Score"—find out how well-positioned your business is for a sale or transfer

Of course, you can always request a consultation with author Noah B. Rosenfarb, CPA. Please call 855-540-0400 x101 to find out about our consultation process.

Made in the USA
Columbia, SC
31 August 2024

2c4579f8-bce3-4608-879d-838c0ca8e588R01